A Name for Your Baby

A Name for Your Baby

Over 10,000 Names
for Boys and Girls
with Nicknames,
Meanings, and Origins

Adrian Room

BARNES
&NOBLE
BOOKS
NEW YORK

This edition published by Marboro Books Corp.,
a division of Barnes & Noble, Inc.,
by arrangement with Adrian Room.

1992 Barnes & Noble Books

Book design by Charles Ziga, Ziga Design

Illustrations by Mary Beth Roberts

ISBN 0-88029-827-8

Printed and bound in the United States of America

M 9 8 7 6 5

Contents

Introduction

How do you go about choosing a name for a baby? Traditionally, this process begins with the necessity of choosing *two* names—one if the baby turns out to be a boy, and another if a girl. While modern science can (by various methods) cut this work in half, expectant parents are still faced with the task of finding a name that will perfectly match the physical attributes and emotional disposition of their child—sight unseen. Is it any wonder they look for help?

A Name for Your Baby aims to provide soon-to-be parents with a wealth of name possibilities. Not only does the book present a wide assortment of names (from the most popular to the unusual), it discusses where the names originated, their literal meanings, and how they have come to be used and reused over the years.

This is not just a book of names. In the introduction, you'll discover many examples of how parents have named their children over the ages. These include names determined by the circumstances of birth, by namesake, and by family tradition. By providing these examples as well as extensive namelists, this book makes it easier than ever for expectant parents to find the perfect name for their baby.

Let's begin with the origin of names.

Names and Their Origins

Like all words in English, names have a language of origin. The following is a list of the sources and languages that have greatly influenced our own, and from which we derive our names.

Classical names. The names of Greek and Roman

mythology are among the oldest we have, yet only a few survive today in regular use. These are, for the most part, short and relatively "simple." In popularity, Alexander is the leader among men, and Helen the most favored among women.

We are not limited to mythological names, however, since the names of real historical figures in classical times have in some cases remained equally in use.

Alexander is one good example—not as just a byname for the mythological Paris—but as the famous Alexander the Great. Names of real classical figures surviving today include the following, mainly a mix of rulers and writers: Anthony (from Mark Antony), Augustus, and Claudius (modern Claude), to name a few.

It is possible to link most classical names with a Latin or Greek word to obtain a literal meaning, although the circumstance of the origin may not be clear. *Cleopatra* thus derives from Greek words literally meaning "father's glory," while *Vergil* has been related (not particularly meaningfully) to Latin *virgo*, "maiden" or *virga*, "stick."

Biblical names. When we read the Bible, we may come across what appears to be a non sequitur. The Book of Genesis provides us with a good example (chapter and verse in parenthesis):

> And the first [child] came out red, all over like an hairy garment; and they [i.e. Isaac and Rebecca] called his name Esau. And after that came his brother out, and his hand took hold on Esau's heel; and his name was called Jacob (25.25–6).

In the original Hebrew, the given name summarizes the circumstances of the child's birth; thus, *Esau* is said to have meant "hairy," and *Jacob* is taken as meaning "heel-grabber." But since the words have been translated (from Hebrew) into English, while the name has not, the particular reference is lost.

While not all biblical names are as easily determined as this, a great many are. And these are the meanings that usually remain associated with the names today. They may not actually be precise—and it is often traditional only—but at least an attempt has been made to link the name with a meaningful word or phrase in its language of origin.

The New Testament has given not just the English-speaking world but the western world in general some of our most familiar names. They are literally "Christian" names, names of members of the early Christian church, and especially (with one notable exception of Judas Iscariot) the names of the disciples of Christ.

These include: Andrew, Elizabeth, James, John, Joseph, Luke, Mark, Martha, Mary, Matthew, Michael (the archangel), Paul, Peter, Philip, Simon, Stephen, Thomas, and Timothy.

Then there are the Old Testament names, almost all of them Hebraic. They include: Aaron, Abigail, Abraham, Adam, Benjamin, Daniel, David, Deborah, Dinah, Esther, Eve, Hannah (modern Ann), Isaac, Isaiah, Jacob, Jeremiah (modern Jeremy), Jesse, Jonathan, Joshua, Leah, Levi, Miriam, Naomi, Rachel, Rebecca, Reuben, Ruth, Samuel, Sarah, Saul, and Solomon.

A few familiar names come from the Apocrypha. These include Judith, Susannah (modern Susan), and Tobias (modern Toby).

Popular names here are David for a man and Deborah, Hannah (as Ann), Rachel, Sarah, or Susan for a woman.

Some of these names, such as Joseph and Michael, occur in both the New and Old Testaments. In the Old Testament, Joseph is Jacob's son; in the New Testament, he is the husband of the Virgin Mary. One or two names are the same: Mary is a form of Miriam, and Simon a form of Simeon. Jesus is actually an Aramaic form of the Hebrew name Joshua.

A further stock of names from the Old Testament was introduced by English-speaking Puritans in the sixteenth and seventeenth centuries. (New Testament names smacked of popery, so were mainly avoided.) Many names of this type were exported to America by Puritan settlers, and biblical names remain prominent in the United States even today.

Celtic and Anglo-Saxon names. Almost as ancient as the classical and biblical names are the names that are Celtic in origin. Those of the Arthurian legends will be mentioned later, but most obviously, Celtic names are the ones that still today are thought of as being specifically Welsh, Scottish, or Irish. *Gwen* is a common Welsh name, *Donald* is Scottish and *Brendan* is Irish, to give only one example for each. In many cases the name as we know it today is a "smoothed" English form of the original. *Gwen* still stands as the Welsh word for "white," or "fair," but *Donald* represents Scottish Gaelic *Domhnall*, comprising the Old Celtic elements *dubno*, "world," and *val*, "rule." Irish *Brendan* represents Irish Gaelic *Bréanainn*, from a Celtic element meaning "prince."

Many English names, however, are more recent than this, and are of Germanic origin, or more specifically Anglo-Saxon. The language spoken by the Angles and Saxons when they invaded England in the fifth century crystallized into what is now usually called Old English. England's earliest kings all have names in this language, and their names typically comprise words or elements that denote power and glory in its many military and personal manifestations.

Anglo-Saxon (Old English) names are frequently

compound by nature, comprising two words or elements. Most of the names beginning *Ed-* are Old English like this, such as Edgar ("riches" + "spear"), Edmund ("riches" + "protector"), Edward ("riches" + "guard"), and Edwin ("riches" + "friend").

To some extent the elements for these names were chosen to link one generation of a family with the previous one, either through repetition of a particular element or even simply through alliteration. Thus St. Wulfstan, eleventh-century bishop of Worcester, was so named as he was the son of Athelstan ("noble" + "stone") and his wife Wulfgifu ("wolf" + "gift"), so that his name meant "wolf" + "stone." While his parents may have hoped for a son who would be brave as a wolf and hard as stone (in other words, a fierce warrior), the origin of the name shows it to have been through sound rather than sense. It is likely that the Anglo-Saxons were as unaware of the literal meanings of their names as most of us are of ours today.

Other influences. Some Germanic names came to England not through the Angles and Saxons but through the Normans (the Norsemen who had settled in France), who introduced them in the eleventh century. Two examples are the names Henry and Richard. Their modern German equivalents, *Heinrich* and *Richard*, indicate their bi-elemental originals more clearly than their present English forms, which have been "smoothed" by the French. *Henry* thus means "home" + "power," and *Richard* means "power" + "brave." (The second half of *Henry* is identical in meaning to the first half of *Richard*.)

Very similar to these are the names that originated from the Scandinavian Vikings, who had also been a presence for centuries. Many Scandinavian names were doublets of Anglo-Saxon names that already existed. *Harold* is a good

example, meaning "army" + "ruler." The Scandinavian
Haraldr is close to Old English *Hereweald*, since both Old
Norse and Old English are commonly Germanic. The
meaning is thus exactly the same in both languages.

Names that are now regarded as pure French, such as
Charles, similarly promoted by the kings who bore them, are
also of Germanic origin. Again, this can be seen through the
modern German equivalents, in this case *Karl*. *Karl* is a
single-element name for once, from a word meaning "free
man" to which the English *churl* is related.

Even some typically Russian names, such as Oleg and
Olga, are of Germanic origin, and originally reached Russia
as Scandinavian imports. These names derive from a
common word meaning "holy," seen in English *holy* itself
(and originally in *hale* in the sense "healthy").

Parents choosing a name for an expected infant
sometimes attach too much importance to its literal
meaning. This is the fault of the popular "naming the baby"
books, which tell you that *Elvis* means "clever friend," or
that *Millicent* means "noble determination." It is almost as if
the parents believe that by calling their baby boy Elvis he
will actually *be* a "clever friend," or that, if the child turns out
to be female after all, their daughter will somehow grow up
to be "nobly determined." It is normally not personally
relevant to boys called *Claude* that they have been dubbed
"lame," or that girls named *Sylvia* are primevally linked with
woodlands.

But in practice, as we all know, people usually choose
and give names for quite different reasons.

Namesakes

One very important reason for giving a particular name is to show admiration for the namesake, whether fictional or historical. This obviously applies to biblical characters, who are themselves a mixture of real and imaginary individuals. (Early figures in the Old Testament are mostly allegorical, while later ones are historical.)

Saints' names. Many New Testament figures are equally well-known as saints. This clearly is an added reason for adopting their names, apart from any special religious association they may have in their own right. The two best-known figures (apart from Jesus) in the New Testament, the Virgin Mary and John the Baptist, are the Christian world's two leading saints and bearers of the two most common names even now. Other Johns and Marys of the faith—at least six of each—give added promotion to the names.

However, there are several saints not appearing as biblical characters, whose names have also become popular. Like their classical and biblical predecessors, some of these saints are historically recognizable figures, while others are probably fictional, or at best are remembered from a highly ornamented "life" that may or may not have been based on that of a real person. Several of the women are "virgin martyrs" who were put to death for their faith in the third or fourth centuries. All the saints mentioned here lived or are dated no later than the eighth century, and most are conventionally placed much earlier than this.

The names themselves are mostly Greek or Latin in origin (with some notable exceptions), showing that the classical naming tradition was the chief one in those years before the Bible was widely known outside its original versions in Greek, Hebrew, and Aramaic. (One of the saints included here, Jerome, who lived in the fourth century, translated most of the Bible into Latin from these tongues.)

There are later saints, of course, some of whom took the names of earlier saints. Others became famous with names hitherto unfamiliar, among them (with the centuries in which they lived) are: Clare (13th), Dominic (13th), Francis (13th), Edmund (13th), Edward (11th), Hugh (11th), Joan (15th), Matilda (13th), Richard (13th), Robert (11th), and Teresa (Theresa) (16th).

This does not mean that people *now* bestow or adopt names with these particular people in mind, but they certainly did so during or soon after their lives. Nor does it mean that the earliest bearer of a name is the true namesake. While the earliest Catherines were named for the (provisionally dated) fourth-century Catherine of Alexandria, bearers of the name in later times may well have been named for the fourteenth-century Catherine of Siena, fifteenth-century Catherine of Genoa, or sixteenth-century Catherine dei Ricci.

Equally, while the earliest saint named Richard lived in the thirteenth century, earlier and more famous uncanonized Richards who were much more likely to have been the original namesakes include the famous twelfth-century king of England Richard I ("Coeur de Lion" or "Lionheart").

Royal names. Names that have been promoted by English kings and queens from the ninth century to the present day include the following, in chronological order (year of death in brackets): Alfred (899), Edward (925), Edmund (946), Edgar (975), Harold (1040), William (1087), Henry (1135), Stephen (1154), Richard (1199), John (1216), Mary (1558), Elizabeth (1603), James (1625), Charles (1649), Anne (1714), George (1727), and Victoria (1901).

Names similarly made known by Scottish kings and

queens include: Malcolm (1093), Donald (1093), Duncan (1094), Alexander (1124), David (1153), Margaret (1290), and Robert (1329).

Some namesakes were particularly noteworthy, such as the first Edward, who was also venerated as a saint; and these did even more to promote the name than sovereigns of lesser lives or shorter reigns. In cases where there were several rulers with the same name, the promotion was continuous down the centuries.

Many royal wives were also familiar to the public. They include: Edith (11th), Matilda (12th), Eleanor (12th), Isabella (14th), Catherine (15th), Margaret (15th), Jane (16th), Henrietta (17th), Caroline (18th), Charlotte (19th), and Alexandra (19th). The names of princes and princesses had a similar impact, especially if they were particularly popular, as Princess Alexandra was.

But to restrict the royal net to Britain is to ignore the influence of many continental European names of sovereigns. The name *Charles* was first and foremost promoted not by Charles I of England but by Charlemagne, back in the eighth century. In fact, many of the English royal names did not originate there but were imported from the continent, such as *William* from Normandy and *George* from Germany.

Surnames. Surnames began their history as additional names (*sur-* meaning "super" or "over and above") added to a single personal name to distinguish one person from another. In some cases a man was described as the son of his father (hence such names as *Johnson*, *Peters*), or as the inhabitant of a particular place (such as *Dale*, who lived in a valley, or *Newton*, who lived in a new settlement). In others a man's name described his occupation (*Taylor*), character (*Stern*), or appearance (*Redhead*). A surname proper evolved when such a name was passed by a man to his son, who himself may not have had any of his father's characteristics. (Women were usually known as the daughter or wife of a respective father or husband.)

Surnames were established in the modern sense of the word in the thirteenth and fourteenth centuries in England, but later in many other countries. In some instances the original name itself became a surname. It then either continued in parallel as a personal name or was adopted as a first name much later, perhaps as recently as the nineteenth century. Examples are *Godfrey* and *Osborn*, now found as both surnames and first names.

The adoption of surnames for first-name use is not new. The practice of giving surnames as first names is characteristic of aristocratic families, and frequently arose through the wish to mark the link by marriage between one noble family and another. Names such as *Cecil*, *Clifford*, and *Dudley* are examples.

Even today, many people (especially males), bear their mother's maiden name as a second or middle name, in some cases adopting it as their actual first name. In fact, where a well-known person has a first name that suggests a surname, it will frequently be found to have actually *been* a surname in the first place. One example is the American poet Robinson Jeffers, whose original name was John Robinson Jeffers.

Since virtually *any* surname can be adopted for first-name use, only the most common surnames-turned-first-names are included in this book.

Men and women of history. In the English-speaking world, there have been many famous men and women who have become namesakes. We should turn first to the heads of state, and in particular to the presidents of the United States of America.

There is little doubt that the names of the earliest U.S. presidents were widely adopted in the New World. George Washington's first name (a typically "English" one, as it turns out), enjoyed wide popularity, as did those of Abraham Lincoln, Theodore Roosevelt, Franklin D. Roosevelt, and Dwight D. Eisenhower. Furthermore, several of the presidents had *surnames* that were taken up as first names. These include: Washington, Jefferson, Monroe, Jackson, Harrison, Lincoln, and Grant.

It is safe to say that *any* first name of an admired public figure, whether truly "great" or simply popular, will often be readily adopted. This applies whether they are statesmen or explorers, military leaders or citizens of historic prominence. For examples one may cite (from each category respectively) Thomas Jefferson, Walter Raleigh, John Paul Jones, and Harriet Tubman or Harriet Beecher Stowe.

Literary exemplars. The names of mythological and biblical characters (allegorical or historical) were mostly promoted through the written or printed word. In a similar fashion, characters in literature can also be in a strong position as namesakes if they are important or in some way unique in their own right.

There are certain areas and types of literature where the characters are particularly memorable, and where their names have consequently passed into general use. One such area is that of the Arthurian romances, which are both classical *and* specifically Christian. They date, in their earliest general appearance, from medieval times, reaching an exquisite literary form in the fifteenth century in Sir Thomas Malory's *Le Morte d'Arthur*, and experienced a popular poetic revival in the nineteenth century from Tennyson's *Idylls of the King*.

The chief name taken from these legends is that of King Arthur. But although Arthur in many ways corresponds to the biblical Jesus (with the Knights of the Round Table as his "disciples"), his name was much more readily adopted.

Other names from the Arthurian romances include Elaine, Enid, Gawain (modern Gavin), Guinevere, Isolde, Merlin, Percival, Tristram, and Vivienne. Oddly, the name of Galahad, most famous of the Knights of the Round Table, has remained almost exclusively unadopted. The name of Modred is also not in standard use.

Most, if not all, of the names of the Arthurian characters are Celtic in origin. They have passed to us through the medium of French, which accounts for their ostensibly Gallic form (especially *Lancelot* and *Percival*).

Shakespeare promoted several new or unfamiliar names in his plays, all female: Bianca, Celia, Charmian, Cordelia, Imogen, Juliet, Miranda, Olivia, Ophelia, and Portia, to name a few. Some of these were probably invented by Shakespeare himself. *Imogen*, however, was the result of a copying error.

In more recent literature, certain first names have been promoted by a whole host of familiar characters. The first name of a central character is sometimes found as the title of a novel, which gives it added prominence, such as *Emma* (Austen), *Lolita* (Nabokov), *Pamela* (Richardson), and *Rebecca* (Du Maurier). (Richardson is credited with the invention of the name Pamela, just as Swift created that of Vanessa.)

If they become "classics," such titles become familiar to people who have never even read the books, but who may be attracted to the name in its own right.

Media names. Today we live not so much in a world of literature as in a "pleasure dome" of movies, shows, radio and television programs, videos, and compact discs. These are sources for many of the names that parents give today.

A good ninety percent of us are exposed to such media almost every day of our lives, so it is hardly surprising that we become aware of names currently in the news. Who, for example, can remain unaware of the names of Gary Cooper, Barbra Streisand, Elvis Presley, or Madonna? Each of these people has an unusual enough name to prompt popular adoption of some kind.

At the beginning of the 1990s, leading names in the fields of popular music and acting included Alyssa Milano, Balthazar Getty, Corey Feldman, Demi Moore, Kiefer Sutherland, Kyle MacLachlan, Kylie Minogue, River Phoenix, Shannen Doherty, and Whitney Houston. (River Phoenix was born to American parents who were members of a religious cult. He has sisters named Rainbow, Liberty, and Summer, and a brother named Leaf. The parents themselves, more prosaically, are John and Arlyn.)

But in the same period there was also the usual leavening of traditional names borne by performers equally in the public eye: Belinda Carlisle, Janet Jackson, Julia Roberts, Michael Jackson, Patrick Swayze, and Paula Abdul.

Naming Patterns

Names go in and out of fashion. One generation may yield a bumper crop of Jeffreys and Jennifers, who in turn may choose the more commonly found names of John and Mary for their own offspring. These waves of fashion are known as naming patterns.

They are not the only patterns, however. Within a family might be a tradition of using the same name for the male

(John Sr., John Jr., John III) or adopting the surname of the mother, as mentioned earlier. The adoption of namesakes certainly follows a pattern, as well.

There are also patterns that convey the impact of certain popular movements. The following categories are examples of some of the most influential of these.

Nature themes. The best-known example is that of names derived from flowers and plants, which came into favor mostly in the latter half of the nineteenth century. These are almost all female names, and include Bryony, Cherry, Daisy, Heather, Ivy, Lily, May, Myrtle, Olive, Rose, and Violet. Many of these are now out of favor; but since Heather is still flourishing, and Bryony blooming, flower names may yet experience a revival.

Another distinct group contains names derived from gems and minerals. (Gemma, although Italian in origin, means "gem" or "jewel" itself.) Names of this type, again all female, include Amber, Crystal, Pearl, and Ruby. Esmeralda also belongs to this group—Spanish and specifically literary in origin, but "emerald" none the less. (The male name Jasper, however, does not fall into this class.)

Names of birds also appear, and include: Linnet, Merle, and Robin. Etymologists will say that the name *Linnet* is actually a diminutive of *Lynn*, and that *Robin*, still chiefly a male name, is a form of *Robert*. But both have been influenced by the bird names, especially for *Robin* in female use.

Modern place-names also provide a select set of first names, while other first names derive from place-names through the medium of surnames, such as Bradford, Montgomery, and Whitney. (Many surnames were imported by the Normans as French place-names. *Montgomery* is only one of these.)

Male-to-female names. Most names divide quite clearly and categorically into male or female. So *Edward* is indisputably male, and *Elizabeth* female. In some cases, however, there has been some "cross-fertilization" of names, usually from male to female. This can happen in one of two ways. Either a male name is adopted as it stands for female use, or a male name is adopted but also adapted for female use, usually with the addition of a traditional female suffix. *Edwin*, for example, becomes female by adding a final -*a* to be *Edwina*, *Justin* adds an -*e* to become *Justine*, and *Claude* can add -*ette* (a French feminine ending) to become *Claudette*. There is also, of course, a female equivalent *Claudia*, but this is a long-established Roman name in its own right, even though, it was in its turn the female equivalent of male *Claudius*.

Names that have been adopted as they stand for female use include *Beverley*, *Hilary*, and *Kimberley*. (The final -*y* may have had something to do with it, suggesting a diminutive or nickname form.) The "takeover" of a name like this does not necessarily mean that it has ceased to be used as a male name. There are still several men named Hilary, but perhaps not so many called Beverley.

In a few instances, however, the adoption has been complete, and some names that were formerly both male and female, or even exclusively male, have become "single-sex" female names.

Many names that are today identical for both sexes have evolved as diminutives of their respective male and female full forms. An example is *Alex*, which can be male or female depending on whether it represents *Alexander* or *Alexandra*. Similarly *Pat* can derive from *Patrick* or *Patricia*.

Variants and diminutives. There is no doubt that many well-established names originated as diminutives (or nickname forms) of a main name. This applies as much to the infant named *Liza* from birth as to the young woman named *Elizabeth* who decides to call herself *Liz*. But that is not to deny their complete independence today; a name may be reserved for private use, among friends and family, but once it is "out in the open," used by the public at large, it is a fully fledged name whatever its origin.

The historic formation of variants and diminutives is an interesting linguistic process. Particularly noteworthy are those diminutives that have not only evolved from a single syllable, but have acquired quite a new consonant in the process. For example, *Richard* gives forth the straightforward *Rich* or *Rick*, while *William* fathers *Will* and *Edward* produces *Ed*. But why should *Richard* have given *Dick*, and *William* produced *Bill*? And how did it come about that *Edward* turned into *Ted*?

The reasons are bound up with the development of the language. *Dick* came about because English speakers in medieval times had difficulty pronouncing the initial trilled *R-* of the Norman name *Richard*. (Ask a Frenchman to say the name today to hear something similar.) The alteration of the consonant in *Bill* is probably due to Gaelic influence. (Compare Irish *balla* and English *wall*. The letters *b* and *w* are not so far removed from each other; since technically, both are voiced labials.) As for *Ted*, the addition is more or less arbitrary. For *Ned*, however, another diminutive of *Edward*, the initial letter derives from *mine Ed*. The same thing happened to *Nan*, originally *mine Ann*.

Nickname or first name? Many media personalities—in particular popular musicians—have first names that are more exactly nicknames, such as *Hoagy* Carmichael, *Chubby* Checker, *Bing* Crosby, *Dizzy* Gillespie, and *Fats* Domino.

For the purposes of this book, such names are not admitted to the general status of first name unless they are widely adopted. Therefore, only generic nicknames such as *Buddy, Chick, Duke, Earl, Red, Sonny, Tiny,* and *Woody,* all of which are fairly widely found, are included among the entries.

Names and associations. Since most names have no meaning in the conventional sense of the word (unlike *chair, class,* or *contribution,* for example), there is a tendency to associate them, and therefore their individual bearers, with like-sounding words. *Andrew,* for example, tends to suggest *hand,* if only through the famous literary *Handy Andy.* Similarly, *Brian* suggests *brain, Bridget* conjures up *bridge,* and *Charmian* evokes *charming.* Some of these word associations are apt, others less so. *Gregory* suggests a person who is *gregarious,* while *Lorna* can seem *forlorn* (which may actually have been the origin of the name).

Through its suggestion of *math, Matthew* seems to imply a brainy person, while *Robert* could be a *robber,* and *Luke* considered *lukewarm.* Even rhyming words may offer themselves, so that *Alice* suggests either *palace* or *malice,* and *Tracy* may be thought "racy" or even "spacy."

Several names have a familiar association with another rhyming word. Thus we have *Plain Jane, Dennis the Menace, Even Steven,* (some of these are children's comic strip characters), *Stormin' Norman* (some are nicknames), and *Clever Trevor.*

Name-givers are recommended to consider such associations when choosing a name.

How to Use This Book

The name entries that follow contain three items of information.

After the name itself comes its **derivation**, with language of origin, where applicable, and literal meaning. In names of Roman origin, a "clan name" is the common name (*nomen*) borne in Roman society by the *gens*, the group of families who were descended in the male line from a single ancestor. (It would have been simpler to call this a "family name," but such a term might suggest that the name was borne only by a single family, instead of a group of families, as was actually the case.) Thus for Julius Caesar, whose full name was Gaius (or Caius) Julius Caesar, his "clan name" was *Julius*, the distinguished patrician *gens* that could be traced back to a single ancestor *Iulus*. Roman women, especially in the "upper classes," did not normally have an individual first name but used the feminine form of their clan name. Hence such names as *Cornelia* (the feminine form of *Cornelius*) and *Claudia* (of *Claudius*), two names still in English-speaking use today.

Where a name has evolved from a surname, the origin of that surname itself is not normally given, unless directly relevant. The literal meaning of a surname rarely has any influence on its suitability for first-name adoption.

The derivation of a first name given in the book is thus almost always the primary one. As some guidance, however, the original nationality of a surname is normally stated, especially where it is not English (that is, where it is specifically Irish, Scottish, or Welsh).

There then follows a brief **history** of the name, giving its time or period of origin and tracing its fortunes since, frequently with reference to a particular country or ethnic provenance. On the whole, women's names are more inventive and innovative than men's, and American and Australian names more original in form and spelling than those in the "Old Country."

The final item of information in the entry is a note on **variants** and **diminutives** of a particular name. Obviously *all* variants and diminutives cannot be given (*Elizabeth* alone has around 50, and *Catherine* almost twice this number), but the chief ones are provided. Some have become popular names in their own right and so have their own independent entries, to which they are cross-referenced. Several names have no regular variants or diminutives, and this fact is similarly stated. Variants or diminutives that do not have their own entry are cross-referenced to the main entry in which they are noted. Identical or near-identical male and female names are similarly cross-referenced from one sex to the other.

It should be stressed that "diminutive" does not necessarily mean a shorter name than the main name. It may be longer, as for *Annie*, the diminutive of *Ann*, or *Nanette*, which has added the French diminutive suffix *-ette* to the name *Nan*. Some books of first names divide secondary names like this into diminutives on the one hand and nicknames on the other. Here they are all diminutives.

On the whole, foreign versions of a name are not included unless they have come to be adopted by English speakers. Examples are French *Marie* and Italian *Maria* as the equivalents of English *Mary*. Both these names are now in English-speaking use.

Additional items of information, such as a guide to a particular name's pronunciation or an indication of its readiness to form a compound with another name, are noted at the appropriate point in the entry.

Boys

Aaran: see **Aaron**

Aaron Biblical name, from Hebrew *Aharōn*, perhaps with root meaning "bright." Spelling variants, such as **Aaran** and **Arn,** irregularly exist, many of them Yiddish.

Abdullah Arabic name, properly *'Abd-Allāh*, "servant of Allah." No recognized variants.

Abe Independently adopted diminutive of **Abraham, Abram,** or (less often), **Abel.** Few regular variants.

Abel Biblical name, from Hebrew *Hebel*, "breath," "vapor," implying vanity. Diminutive, **Abe,** exists independently.

Abner Biblical name, from Hebrew *'Abnēr,* "father of light" (i.e., God). Diminutive variant, **Abe,** sometimes found in independent use.

Abraham Biblical name, from Hebrew *Abrāham*, representing *av hamon* (*goyim*), "father of a multitude (of nations)." Yiddish variant spelling is **Avrom.** Usual diminutive is **Abe,** in independent use.

Abram Biblical name, from Hebrew *Abrām*, "high father," but now usually regarded as contracted form of **Abraham.** Variants as for Abraham, with same standard diminutive, **Abe,** in independent use.

Absalom Biblical name, from Hebrew *Abshālōm*, "father of peace" (i.e., God). Few regular variants.

Achilles Greek name, traditionally said to mean "lipless," from *a-*, "without" or "not," and *kheile*, "lips," as famous Achilles of Greek mythology had never been suckled. However, name is probably pre-Greek in origin. No regular variants.

Ad: see **Adrian**

Adam Biblical name, from Hebrew *'ādām*, "human being" or "man." Occasional irregular spelling variants, with Scottish diminutive, **Adie**, sometimes found.

Ade: see **Adrian**

Adie: see **Adam**

Adolf: see **Adolph**

Adolph From Old German name *Adalwolf*, from *adal*, "noble," and *wolf*, "wolf": "noble wolf." Variant, **Adolf**, is modern German spelling, notorious from Nazi dictator Adolf Hitler (1889–1945). French variant, **Adolphe**, was promoted by French-American actor Adolphe Menjou (1890–1963). **Adolphus** is independently adopted variant. Diminutive, **Dolly**, sometimes found.

Adolphe: see **Adolph**

Adolphus Latin-style variant of **Adolph**, adopted independently. Diminutive, **Dolly**, exists.

Adonis Greek name, from Phoenician *adon*, "lord" (compare to *Adonai*, Judaic title of God). No regular variants, if any at all.

Adrian English form of Latin name *Hadrianus*, "man of Adria" (town in northern Italy that gave the Adriatic Sea its name). Most common diminutive variants are **Ad** and **Ade**.

Aeneas Greek name, traditionally derived from *ainein*, "to praise." No regular variants.

Ahmad: see **Ahmed**

Ahmed Arabic name, from *ahmad*, "more praiseworthy," itself from *hamida*, "to praise." Compare **Muhammad.** Variant spelling, **Ahmad**, sometimes found, as for jazz musician Ahmad Jamal (born 1930).

Aidan English form of Gaelic name *Aodán*, itself a diminutive of *Aodh*, "fire." No regular variants.

Al Independently adopted diminutive of **Albert, Alexander, Alfred, Alvin**, and any name beginning *Al-*. Diminutive variants, **Allie** and **Ally**, exist.

Alan Celtic name, traditionally derived from *alun*, "harmony" or "concord." Variant spellings, **Allan** and **Allen** exist, while Welsh form is **Alun**. Diminutive, **Al**, is in independent use.

Alastair English form of Gaelic *Alasdair*, itself a form of **Alexander**. Alternate spelling, **Alistair,** also popular, as for British-American radio journalist Alistair Cooke (born 1909). Further variant, **Alister**, sometimes found. Diminutive, **Aly**, is fairly common.

Albert Old German name, *Adalbert*, from *adal*, "noble," and *beraht*, "bright" or "famous": "noble and famous." Best-known variants are independently adopted diminutives, **Al** and **Bert**.

Aldous Probably based on Old German *ald*, "old." No regular variants.

Alec Independently adopted diminutive of **Alexander.** Variant, **Alex**, is in independent use. Rare variant, **Aleck**, occurs.

Aleck: see **Alec**

Alex Independently adopted diminutive of **Alexander**. **Alec** is directly related variant, and diminutive, **Lex**, is sometimes found.

Alexander Greek name, from *alexein*, "to defend," and *anēr*, genitive *andros*, "man": "defender of men." Variant diminutives, **Alec**, **Alex**, and **Sandy**, are in independent use. **Alick** is also found.

Alf Independently adopted diminutive of **Alfred**. Usual diminutive variant is **Al**, in independent use, but **Alfie** also exists.

Alfie: see **Alf**

Alfonso: see **Alphonse**

Alfred From Old English name *Ælfrǣd*, comprising *ælf*, "elf," and *rǣd*, "counsel": "elf counsel" or "inspired advice." Diminutive variants, **Al**, **Alf**, and **Fred**, are in independent use.

Algernon Norman French name, from *als gernons*, "with whiskers," arising as nickname for moustached or bewhiskered man. Usual diminutive is **Algie** or **Algy**.

Algie: see **Algernon**

Algy: see **Algernon**

Alick: see **Alexander**

Alistair: see **Alastair**

Alister: see **Alastair**

Allan: see **Alan**

Allen: see **Alan**

Allie: see **Al**

Ally: see **Al**

Alois: see **Aloysius**

Alonso Smoothed form of Spanish *Alfonso* (**Alphonse**). Alternate spelling, **Alonzo**, exists, and diminutive, **Al**, is in independent use.

Alonzo: see **Alonso**

Aloysius Perhaps Latinized form of **Louis**. German variant, **Alois**, sometimes found, with diminutive, **Al**, in independent use.

Alphonse French form of Spanish *Alfonso*, itself of Old German origin, comprising *adal*, "noble," or *hild*, "battle," and *funs*, "ready": "noble and ready" or "battle-ready." **Alfonso** itself is alternate spelling, and usual diminutive is **Al**, in independent use.

Alfonso: see **Alphonse**

Alun: see **Alan**

Alvin Old English name *Ælfwine*, comprising *ælf*, "elf," and *wine*, "friend": "elf friend," implying supernatural support. Many variant spellings, often with *w*, as **Alwyn**. Usual diminutive is **Al**, in independent use.

Alwyn: see **Alvin**

Aly: see **Alastair**

Ambrose English form of Latin name *Ambrosius*, itself from Greek *ambrosios*, "immortal." Few regular variants.

Amias: see **Amyas**

Aminadab Biblical name, from Hebrew *'Ammīnādāb*, "my people (are) generous." No regular variants.

Amos Biblical name, from Hebrew *Āmōs*, "borne." Few regular variants.

Amyas Perhaps form of Latin name *Amatus*, "loved," influenced by French *aimé*, in same sense. Variant spelling, **Amias**, also exists.

Anatole French name, from Latin name *Anatolius*, itself from Greek *anatolē*, "sunrise" or "east." Few regular variants.

André French form of **Andrew**. No regular variants.

Andrew Biblical name, from Greek *Andreas*, from *anēr*, genitive *andros*, "man": "manly" or "brave." French version of name, **André**, exists in independent use, as does Scottish diminutive, **Drew**. Regular diminutive is **Andy**, in independent use.

Andy Independently adopted diminutive of **Andrew**. Few regular variants.

Aneirin: see **Aneurin**

Aneurin Welsh name, perhaps from Welsh *an*, "all," and *eur*, "gold," with diminutive suffix *-in*: figuratively, "very precious little one." (Middle vowel is pronounced as in "nigh.") Older spelling, **Aneirin**, still in use. Usual diminutive is **Nye**.

Angel From Latin name *Angelus*, itself from Greek *angelos*, literally "messenger," but in New Testament as "messenger of God." See also female version, **Angel**. No regular variants.

Angelo Italian or Spanish form of Latin name, *Angelus* (**Angel**). Few regular variants.

Angie: see **Angus**

Angus English form of Gaelic name *Aonghus*, comprising *aon*, "one," and *ghus*, "choice": "sole choice," implying uniqueness. Diminutive variant, **Gus**, is in independent use, and **Angie** (with hard "g"), also exists.

Anselm Old German name *Anshelm*, comprising *ans*, "god," and *helm*, "helmet": "divinely protected." Few regular variants.

Anthony English form of Roman clan name *Antonius*, itself of uncertain origin. Insertion of *h* due to association with Greek *anthos*, "flower."

Archibald From Norman French name *Archambault*, itself from Old German name comprising *erkan*, "genuine," and *bald*, "bold": "truly brave." Regular diminutives are **Archie** and **Archy.**

Archie: see **Archibald**

Archy: see **Archibald**

Ariel Biblical name, from Hebrew *Arī'ēl*, "lion of God." Few variants in regular use.

Arn: see **Aaron** and **Arnold**

Arnie: see **Arnold**

Arnold From Old German name *Arinwald*, comprising *arn*, "eagle," and *wald*, "ruler: "eagle-ruler." Diminutives include: **Arn** and **Arnie.**

Art Independently adopted diminutive of **Arthur.** Diminutive, **Artie,** also exists.

Arthur Celtic name of uncertain origin, but linked with *art*, "bear." (Compare similar link between Arctic, from Greek *arktos*, "bear," and constellation of Ursa Major, or Great Bear, under which Arctic lies.) Diminutive variant, **Art**, is in independent use.

Artie: see **Art**

Asa Biblical name, from Hebrew *Āsā*, "healer," (originally a nickname). No regular variants.

Asher Biblical name, from Hebrew *Āshēr*, "happy." No regular variants.

Ashley From the surname. Few regular variants.

Athelstan From Old English name *Æthelstān*, comprising *æthele*, "noble," and *stān*, "stone": "nobly strong." No regular variants.

Auberon: see **Aubrey**

Aubrey From French version of Old German name *Alberich*, comprising *alb*, "elf," and *rīc*, "power": so "supernaturally powerful." Possible variant is **Auberon**.

Augustin: see **Augustine**

Augustine English form of Latin name *Augustinus*, diminutive of **Augustus**. Spelling variant, **Augustin**, is common, and contracted form, **Austin**, is independent name. Regular diminutive is **Gus**, in independent use.

Augustus Latin name, from standard word *augustus*, "great" or "august," adopted as title by Roman emperors. **Augustine** is related name, as is **Austin**. Regular diminutive is **Gus**, in independent use.

Austin Originally contracted form of **Augustine**, but now often adoption of surname, **Austin,** for first-name use. Spelling variant, **Austen,** is common.

Avery From surname, itself from medieval form of **Alfred.** No established variants.

Avrom: see **Abraham**

Aylmer From Old English name *Æthelmǽr,* comprising *æthele,* "noble," and *mǽre,* "famous": "nobly famed." Also an adoption of surname. No regular variants.

Azariah Biblical name, from Hebrew *'Azaryāh,* "helped by God." No regular variants.

Baldwin From French version of Old German name *Baldawin*, comprising *bald*, "bold" or "brave," and *wine*, "friend": "brave friend" or "comrade-in-arms." Few regular variants.

Balthasar: see **Balthazar**

Balthazar Variant of name of biblical king Belshazzar, ultimately from Babylonian *Bēl-sharra-usur*, "Bel protect the king" (Bel being the supreme deity). Variant spelling, **Balthasar**, is frequent. Diminutive, **Balty**, exists.

Balty: see **Balthazar**

Bamber From surname. No variants.

Bardolph From Old German name *Bartholf*, comprising *beraht*, "bright," or *barta*, "ax," and *wolf*, "wolf": "famous wolf" or "ax wolf," with the latter implying ferocity. No regular variants.

Barnabas Biblical name, from Aramaic *Barněbhū'āh*, "son of consolation." Diminutive variant, **Barney**, is in independent use.

Barnaby Spoken form of **Barnabas** evolved in medieval times. Diminutive variant, **Barney**, exists independently.

Barney Independently adopted diminutive of **Barnabas** or **Barnaby**. Variant spelling, **Barny**, occurs.

Barny: see **Barney**

Barry Either English form of Irish name *Barra*, short form of *Fionnbarr*, itself comprising Irish *fionn*, "white" or "fair," and *barr*, "head," or else direct from Irish *bearach*, "spear." Diminutives are **Baz** and **Bazza** (especially in Australia).

Bart: see **Bartholomew**

Bartholomew Biblical name, from Aramaic formation meaning "son of Talmai" (latter is also biblical name, from Hebrew meaning "abounding in furrows"). Regular diminutive is **Bart**.

Baruch Biblical name, from Hebrew *Bārūk*, "blessed" (compare to **Benedict**). No regular variants.

Bas: see **Basil**

Basil From Greek name *Basileios*, meaning "royal," itself from *basileus*, "king." Diminutives, **Bas** and **Baz**, exist.

Baz: see **Barry, Basil,** and **Sebastian**

Bazza: see **Barry** and **Sebastian**

Beau From standard nickname, meaning "handsome." No established variants.

Ben Independently adopted diminutive of **Benjamin**, or (less frequently), **Benedict**. **Benny** exists as diminutive in own right.

Benedick: see **Benedict**

Benedict From Latin name *Benedictus*, "blessed." Rare variant is **Benedick**. Diminutive, **Ben**, can occur independently.

Benjamin Biblical name, from Hebrew *Binyāmīn*, "son of the right hand," implying favorite. **Ben** and **Benny** are diminutives in independent use. Others include **Benjie** and **Benjy**.

Benjie: see **Benjamin**

Benjy: see **Benjamin**

Bennie: see **Benny**

Benny Independently adopted diminutive of **Benjamin** or **Ben**. Alternate spelling, **Bennie**, also occurs, as for jazzman Bennie Green (1923–1977).

Bernard Either from Old English name *Beornheard*, comprising *beorn*, "man" or "warrior," and *heard*, "brave," or from Old German *Berinhard*, comprising *ber*, "bear," and *hart*, "bold" or "stern." Regular diminutive is **Bernie**, with **Bunny** sometimes found in independent use.

Bernie: see **Bernard**

Bert Independently adopted diminutive of **Albert**, or (less commonly), **Bertram**. Variant spelling, **Burt**, exists, while regular diminutive is **Bertie**, both adopted in own right.

Bertie Independently adopted diminutive of **Bert**, **Albert**, or **Bertram**. Few further variants.

Bertram From French version of Old German name *Berahtram*, comprising *beraht*, "bright" or "famous," and *hramn*, "raven": "famous raven," implying wise person. **Bertrand** is variant in own right. Usual diminutives are independently adopted **Bert** or **Bertie**.

Bertrand Independently adopted variant of **Bertram**. Variant diminutive, **Bertie**, occurs.

Bev: see **Beverley**

Beverley From surname, itself from town in Yorkshire. Compare to female name **Beverly**. Diminutive, **Bev**, occurs.

Bevis From surname (now more commonly Beavis). (Pronunciation is with short or long *e*.) No regular variants.

Bill Diminutive of **William**, adopted for independent use. Diminutive, **Billy**, is in independent use.

Billie: see **Billy**

Billy Independent adoption of diminutive of **William** (and later of **Bill**). Variant spelling, **Billie**, also exists. Compare to female name **Billie**.

Boaz Biblical name of Hebrew origin, perhaps meaning "swiftness." No regular variants.

Bob Independently adopted diminutive of **Robert**. Variant diminutive is **Bobby**, also in independent use.

Bobbie: see **Bobby**

Bobby Independently adopted diminutive of **Bob**, or directly of **Robert**. Spelling variant, **Bobbie**, also exists.

Boris Russian name, popularly derived from Slavic root *bor-* meaning "fight" or "struggle," but possibly Tartar nickname meaning "small." No regular variants.

Boyd From Scottish surname. No regular variants.

Brad: see **Bradley**

Bradley From surname. Diminutive variant, **Brad**, is fairly common.

Brandon From surname, but doubtlessly influenced by **Brendan**. Diminutive variant, **Brandy**, exists.

Brandy: see **Brandon**

Brendan English version of Irish name *Bréanainn*, based on Gaelic word meaning "prince." Few regular variants.

Brent From surname, perhaps influenced by **Brett**. No regular variants.

Brett From surname. No established variants.

Bri: see **Brian**

Brian English version of Irish name perhaps based on Celtic *brigh*, "power." Alternate spelling, **Bryan**, is in independent use. Diminutive, **Bri**, occurs.

Brook From surname. Diminutive, **Brookie**, is sometimes found.

Brookie: see **Brook**

Bruce From Scottish surname, famous from fourteenth-century king of Scotland, Robert "the Bruce." Variant diminutive, **Brucie**, is fairly general.

Brucie: see **Bruce**

Bruno From Old German name based on *brun*, "brown," implying brown hair, eyes, skin, or perhaps, simply bearlike. No regular variants.

Bry: see **Bryan**

Bryan Independently adopted variant spelling of **Brian**. Diminutive, **Bry**, occurs.

Buck From nickname, itself from "buck" (male deer or he-goat), often applied to lively young man. No regular variants.

Bud From standard nickname for a friend, itself short form of "buddy." Variant, **Buddy**, is in independent use.

Buddy From standard nickname for a friend. No regular variants, although **Bud** is directly related.

Bunny Either independently adopted diminutive of **Bernard** or **Henry**, or nickname for "rabbit" or other associations. No regular variants.

Burt Either variant spelling of **Bert** or independently adopted diminutive of **Burton**. No established variants.

Burton From surname. Regular variant diminutive is **Burt**, used independently.

Buster From nickname for active or simply unfamiliar person. No established variants.

Butch From nickname, usually for stocky or tough person (in origin from "butcher"). No regular variants.

Byron From surname. Few established variants.

Cadwalader Welsh name, comprising *cad*, "battle," and *gwaladr*, "disposer," implying one who deploys troops for battle. Variant spelling, **Cadwallader**, exists.

Cadwallader: see **Cadwalader**

Caesar From Latin imperial family name, or modern equivalent, such as French *César*, Italian *Cesare*. Few established variants, although irregular spellings of name occur.

Cal: see **Calvin**

Caleb Biblical name, from Hebrew *kālēb*, "dog," perhaps implying devotion to God. No established variants.

Calvin From French surname, made famous by French Protestant theologian Jean Calvin (1509–1564). Diminutive variant, **Cal**, is in regular use.

Cameron From Scottish clan name and surname. No regular variants.

Caradoc Version of Welsh name *Caradog*, itself based on Welsh root element *car-*, "love." No variants in regular use.

Carey: see **Cary**

Carl Alternate spelling of German *Karl* (**Charles**). Italian form of name, **Carlo**, also found in English-speaking use, as is now original **Karl**.

Carlo: see **Carl**

Carol English form of Latin *Carolus* (**Charles**). Spelling variant, **Carroll**, is more common as independent name. Slavic form, **Karel**, is also found.

Carroll Independently adopted variant of **Carol**, with spelling distinguishing from female name, **Carol**. No regular variants.

Cary From surname. Variant spelling, **Carey**, occurs, as borne by American playwright Carey Harrison.

Casey Either from Irish surname, or direct from American folk hero and railroad engineer Casey Jones (1863–1900). Sometimes spelled **Kasey**.

Caspar From Dutch version of **Jasper**. Variant spellings, **Casper**, **Kaspar**, and **Kasper** occur.

Casper: see **Caspar**

Cass: see **Cassius**

Cassie: see **Cassius**

Cassius From Roman clan name, of uncertain derivation (but possibly connected with Latin *cassus*, "empty"). Diminutive variants, **Cass** and **Cassie**, exist.

Cat From nickname, for the animal (referring to fiery temper and the like) or as "hep-cat." No established variants.

Cecil Originally English form of Roman clan name *Caecilius*, from nickname *Caecus*, "blind," but later from surname, famous as that of sixteenth-century noble English family. No regular variants.

Cedric Variant of *Cerdic*, name of traditional founder of Wessex. No established variants.

Chad Modern English version of Old English *Ceadda*,

perhaps based on Celtic *cad*, "battle," (compare to **Cadwalader**). No established variants.

Charles Ultimately from Old German word *karl*, "man," implying bravery or freedom of action (compare to Old English *ceorl*, "countryman," modern "churl" and "churlish"). Stock diminutive variant is **Charlie**, with **Chas** also now widely found. Diminutives **Chick** and **Chuck** are used independently in the U.S.

Charlie: see **Charles**

Charlton From surname. Few established variants.

Chas: see **Charles**

Ches: see **Chesney**

Chesney From surname. Diminutive variant, **Chet**, is in independent use. **Ches** also exists.

Chester From surname. Variant diminutive, **Chet**, is in independent use.

Chet Independently adopted diminutive of **Chesney** and **Chester**. No regular variants.

Chick Either independently adopted diminutive of **Charles** or as nickname for young or small person. No regular variants.

Chris Independently adopted diminutive of **Christopher**, or (less commonly), **Christian**. Compare to female name, **Christine**. Variant spelling, **Kris**, exists, as for musician/ songwriter Kris Kristofferson (born 1936).

Christian From Latin name *Christianus*, "follower of Christ." Regular diminutive variant is **Chris**, in independent use.

Christie: see **Christy**

Christmas Either from surname or directly for the holiday (compare to **Noël**). No regular variants, though diminutive, **Chris**, could logically evolve.

Christopher From Greek name *Khristophoros*, comprising *Khristos*, "Christ," and *pherein*, "to bear": "bearing Christ" (that is, in the heart), although sometimes popularly interpreted as "borne by Christ." Regular diminutive variants in independent use are **Chris** and **Christy**.

Christy Independently adopted diminutive of **Christopher**. Spelling variant, **Christie**, also widely found.

Chuck Either from standard nickname for friend (term of endearment), or as independently adopted diminutive of **Charles**. Variant diminutive, **Chuckie**, fairly common.

Chuckie: see **Chuck**

Clancy Either from Irish surname, or independently adopted diminutive of **Clarence**. No regular variants.

Clarence Essentially adopted from Duke of Clarence (1864–1892), elder son of Edward VII, whose title dates back to fourteenth century and ultimately derives from placename Clare, Suffolk. Usual diminutive variant is **Clarrie**, but **Clancy** also found.

Clark From surname. Occasional spelling variant, **Clarke**, occurs.

Clarke: see **Clark**

Clarrie: see **Clarence**

Claud: see **Claude**

Claude From Roman clan name *Claudius*, itself from

nickname *Claudus*, "lame." Variant spelling, **Claud**, is frequent alternate spelling.

Clem: see **Clement**

Clement From Latin name *Clemens*, genitive *Clementis*, meaning "merciful" (modern English "clement"). Regular diminutive variant is **Clem**.

Cliff Independently adopted diminutive of **Clifford**, or (less often), **Clifton**, also associated with standard word "cliff" or with name Clive. Few regular variants.

Clifford From surname. Regular diminutive is **Cliff**, in independent use.

Clifton From surname. Regular diminutive is **Cliff**, in independent use.

Clint Independently adopted diminutive of surname **Clinton**. Few regular variants.

Clive From surname. No established variants.

Clovis Latinized form of French name **Louis**. No regular variants, but **Ludovic** is directly related name.

Clyde From placename, a river in southwest Scotland. No regular variants.

Colin Either independently adopted diminutive of Nicholas, or (less frequently), English form of Scottish name *Cailean*, "whelp" or "puppy" (compare to English "collie"). Few established variants.

Con: see **Conrad** and **Constant**

Connie: see **Conrad** and **Constant**

Conrad English spelling of German *Konrad*, comprising Old German *kuon*, "bold," and *rad*, "counsel": "bold counsel." Diminutive variants, **Con** and **Connie**, occur.

Constant From Latin name *Constans*, genitive *Constantis*, "steadfast" or "constant." Diminutive variants, **Con** and **Connie**, occasionally occur.

Constantine From Latin name *Constantinus*, derivative of *Constans* (**Constant**). No regular variants.

Corey From surname. No regular variants.

Cornelius Biblical name, from Roman clan name *Cornelius*, of uncertain origin (but perhaps connected with *cornu*, "horn"). Diminutive variants, **Corney** and **Corny**, sometimes occur.

Corney: see **Cornelius**

Corny: see **Cornelius**

Cosmo From Italian form of Greek name *Kosmas*, itself based on *kosmos*, "order" or "beauty" (compare to English "cosmic"). No established variants.

Courteney From surname. Alternate spelling, **Courtney**, also occurs.

Courtney: see **Courteney**

Craig From surname, itself Scottish placename to which English "crag" relates. No regular variants.

Crispin From Latin name *Crispinus*, derivative of Roman clan name *Crispus*, itself nickname meaning "curly-haired." No regular variants.

Cuddie: see **Cuthbert**

Curt: see **Kurt**

Curtis From surname. Few established variants.

Cuthbert From Old English name *Cuthbeorht*, comprising *cūth*, "known," and *beorht*, "bright" or "famous": "well-known." Diminutive, **Bert**, is in independent use, and **Cuddie** is also found in Scotland.

Cy Independently adopted diminutive of **Cyrus**. No established variants.

Cyprian From Latin name *Cyprianus*, "man of Cyprus." No established variants.

Cyril From Greek name *Kyrillos*, itself based on *kyrios*, "lord." Few regular variants.

Cyrus Biblical name, from Greek name *Kyros*, that of several kings of Persia, itself of unknown origin but associated with Greek *kyrios*, "lord" (as for **Cyril**). Regular variant diminutive is **Cy**, in independent use.

Dai Welsh name, originally from Old Celtic *dei*, "to shine," but now regarded as independently adopted diminutive of **David**. No regular variants.

Dale From surname. No regular variants.

Damian From Greek *Damianos*, in turn from *damān*, "to tame" or "to subdue": "tamer." **Damon** is directly related name.

Damon Independently adopted variant of **Damian**. No established variants.

Dan Both biblical name, from Hebrew *Dān*, "judge," and independently adopted diminutive of **Daniel**.

Dana From surname, or as variant of **Daniel**. Compare to female name **Dana**. No established variants.

Dane From surname, itself a variant of **Dean**. **Dana** is sometimes regarded as variant in independent use.

Daniel Either biblical name, from Hebrew *Dāni'el*, "God is my judge," or English form of Irish name *Domhnall* (**Donald**). Diminutive variants, **Dan** and **Danny**, are in independent use.

Danny Independently adopted diminutive of **Daniel**. Further diminutive, **Dan**, is also in independent use.

Darcy From Norman surname. Compare to female name **Darcey**. Few regular variants.

Darrell From surname. Apparent variant, **Darryl**, may be distinct name.

Darren Apparently alteration of **Darrell**, later associated with the female names **Karen** and **Sharon**. Few established variants.

Darryl Either from surname or as independently adopted variant of **Darrell**, with spelling perhaps prompted by name such as **Cheryl**. Variant spelling, **Daryl**, is in independent use.

Daryl Independently adopted spelling variant of **Darryl**. Few established variants.

Dave Independently adopted diminutive of **David**. Variant, **Davy**, is also in independent use.

Davey: see **Davy**

David Biblical name, from Hebrew *Dāwid*, perhaps meaning "favorite." Regular diminutive variants, **Dave** and **Davy**, are in independent use.

Davie: see **Davy**

Davy Independently adopted diminutive of **David**. Can also serve as diminutive (or variant) of **Dave**, and has alternate spellings, **Davey** and **Davie**.

Dean From surname, but also having association with standard word, implying status. Variant spelling, **Deane**, occurs. **Dane** and **Dana** are regarded as variants in independent use.

Deane: see **Dean**

Declan English form of Irish name *Deaglán*, of unknown origin. No regular variants.

Del: see **Derek**

Delbert Apparently modification of names such as **Albert** and **Robert**. Few regular variants.

Den: see **Dennis**

Denis Independently adopted variant of **Dennis**. No regular variants.

Dennis From medieval spoken form of Greek name *Dionysios*, given to one who revered this classical god of wine, whose own name is probably related to that of *Zeus*. Alternate spelling, **Denis**, is found independently, although not as often. Regular diminutive is **Den**.

Denzil From Cornish surname. No established variants.

Derek English form of original German name *Theodoric* (which also gave **Terry**), itself meaning "ruler of the people." Variant spelling, **Derrick**, also exists. Regular diminutive is **Del**.

Dermot English form of Irish name *Diarmaid*, itself of uncertain origin, but perhaps combining *di*, "without," and *airmait*, "envy." No regular variants.

Derrick: see **Derek**

Des: see **Desmond**

Desmond From Irish surname, with spelling apparently influenced by **Esmond**. Regular diminutive is **Des**.

Dex: see **Dexter**

Dexter From surname. Usual diminutive variant is **Dex**.

Dick Independently adopted diminutive of **Richard**. Diminutive forms, **Dickie** and **Dicky**, are common.

Dickie: see **Dick**

Dicky: see **Dick**

Diggory Origin uncertain, but possibly derived from name born by central character of medieval romance *Sir Degaré*, itself perhaps corruption of French *l'esgaré*, "the lost one." Variant spelling, **Digory**, exists.

Digory: see **Diggory**

Dion Shortened form of Greek name such as *Dionysius* (see **Dennis**). No regular variants.

Dirk Dutch form of **Derek**, popularly associated with standard word for Scottish dagger. No established variants.

Dolly: see **Adolph** and **Adolphus**

Dominic From Latin name *Dominicus*, itself based on *dominus*, "lord." Variant spelling, **Dominick**, is sometimes found.

Dominick: see **Dominic**

Don Independently adopted diminutive of **Donald** or **Donovan**. Diminutive variant, **Donny**, is in independent use.

Donald English form of Gaelic name *Domhnall*, comprising Celtic *dubno*, "world," and *val*, "rule": "powerful worldwide." (Final -d of name is by association with names such as **Dugald**.) Standard diminutive variant is **Don**, in independent use.

Donny Independently adopted diminutive of **Donald**, **Donovan**, and **Don**. No established variants.

Donovan From Irish surname originally used as first name, itself meaning "dark brown," referring to color of hair, eyes, or skin. Regular diminutive variant is **Don**, used independently.

Dorian From Latin name *Dorius*, in turn from Greek name meaning "Dorian" (from Doris, ancient region of central Greece). Now sometimes felt to be the male equivalent of **Doris**, with ending influenced by names such as **Adrian** and **Julian**. No regular variants.

Doug: see **Dougal** and **Douglas**

Dougal English form of Gaelic name *Dubhgall*, comprising *dubh*, "black," and *gall*, "stranger." (Said to have been Irish nickname for dark-haired Danes, as compared to blond Norwegians and Icelanders.) Variant diminutives are **Doug** and **Dougie**.

Dougie: see **Dougal** and **Douglas**

Douglas From Scottish surname, but now associated with **Dougal**. Regular diminutive variant is **Doug**, with **Dougie**, **Dug**, and **Duggie** also found.

Drew Independently adopted diminutive of **Andrew**, though sometimes popularly associated with surname. No regular variants.

Duane English version of Gaelic name *Dubhán*, itself diminutive form of *dubh*, "black": "little black-haired one." Variant spelling, **Dwayne**, exists.

Dud: see **Dudley**

Dudley From surname. Regular diminutive is **Dud**.

Dug: see **Dougald** and **Douglas**

Dugald Independently adopted variant of **Dougal**, with final -d by association with such names as **Arnold**. Variant diminutives, **Dug** and **Duggie**, sometimes occur.

Duggie: see **Dugald** and **Douglas**

Duke Either independently adopted diminutive of **Marmaduke**, or from surname, or adoption of nickname (as for **Earl** or **King**). Few established variants.

Duncan English form of Gaelic name *Donnchadh*, comprising Old Celtic *donn*, "dark," and *cath*, "battle": "dark-haired warrior." Diminutive variants, **Dunk**, **Dunkie**, and **Dunky**, occur.

Dunk: see **Duncan**

Dunkie: see **Duncan**

Dunky: see **Duncan**

Dunstan From placename or surname. Few established variants.

Dustin From surname, perhaps influenced by names such as **Austen** and **Justin**. No established variants.

Dwayne: see **Duane**

Dwight From surname. No regular variants.

Dylan Welsh name, probably based on Celtic root word meaning "sea," to which modern Welsh *dylif*, "flood," is related. No regular variants, but diminutive, **Dyl**, is possible.

Eamon Irish form of **Edmund**. Alternate spelling, **Eamonn**, exists.

Eamonn: see **Eamon**

Earl From aristocratic title used as nickname (as for **Duke**, **King**, or **Prince**) or from surname. Variant spelling, **Erle**, familiar from detective fiction writer Erle Stanley Gardner (1889–1970).

Eben: see **Ebenezer**

Ebenezer Biblical name (but that of place, not person), from Hebrew *eben-ha'ēzer*, "stone of help." Diminutive variant, **Eben**, exists.

Ed Independently adopted diminutive of **Edgar**, **Edmund**, **Edward** (commonly), or **Edwin**. Diminutive variant, **Eddie**, occurs in own right.

Eddie Independently adopted diminutive of **Ed** or of names that give that diminutive, such as **Edgar**, **Edmund**, and **Edward**. Variant spelling, **Eddy**, occurs, as for country singer Eddy Arnold (born 1918).

Eddy: see **Eddie**, **Edgar**, **Edmund**, and **Edward**

Eden Either from surname, or from biblical name (but of place, not person), from Hebrew *'ēden*, "delight" or "paradise." No regular variants.

Edgar From Old English name *Ēadgār*, comprising *ēad*,

"prosperity" or "riches," and *gār*, "spear": "owning many spears." Diminutive variants, **Ed** (in independent use), **Eddie**, and **Eddy**, occur.

Edmond: see **Edmund**

Edmund From Old English name *Ēadmund*, comprising *ēad*, "prosperity" or "riches," and *mund*, "protector": "wealth protector." Variant spelling, **Edmond**, is increasingly frequent, as for Anglo-Irish actor Edmond O'Brien (1915–1985). Regular diminutives are **Ed** (in independent use), **Eddie**, and **Eddy**.

Edward From Old English name *Ēadweard*, comprising *ēad*, "prosperity" or "riches," and *weard*, "guard": "wealth guardian." Variant diminutives, **Ed**, **Ned**, and **Ted**, are in independent use. Also common are, **Eddie** and **Eddy**.

Edwin From Old English name *Ēadwine*, comprising *ēad*, "prosperity" or "riches," and *wine*, "friend": "friend of riches." Spelling variant, **Edwyn**, sometimes found, with regular diminutive, **Ed**, independently used.

Edwyn: see **Edwin**

Effie: see **Ephraim**

Egbert From Old English name *Ecgbeorht*, comprising *ecg*, "edge" (of a sword), and *beorht*, "bright" or "famous": "famous swordsman." No regular variants, although **Bert** would be expected diminutive.

Eldred From Old English name *Ealdred*, comprising *eald*, "old," and *rǣd*, "counsel," so "longstanding counsel." No variants.

Eli Biblical name, from Hebrew *'Elī*, "high." Few regular variants.

Elias Greek form of **Elijah**. Few established variants.

Elijah Biblical name, from Hebrew *Ēlīyāhū*, "God is Yah" (i.e., Jehovah). Greek variant of name, **Elias**, is in independent use. Yiddish diminutive, **Elye**, occurs.

Eliot: see **Elliott**

Eliott: see **Elliott**

Eliphalet Biblical name, from Hebrew *Ēlīphelet*, "God is release." No regular variants.

Elisha Biblical name, from Hebrew *Ēlīshā*, "God is salvation." No established variants.

Elliot: see **Elliott**

Elliott From surname (more usual as **Eliot**). Spelling variants, **Eliot**, **Eliott**, and **Elliot**, exist.

Elm: see **Elmer**

Elmer From surname. Diminutive variants, **Elm** and **Elmy**, occur.

Elmy: see **Elmer**

Elroy Variant of **Leroy**. Few fixed variants.

Elton From surname. No regular variants.

Elvis Perhaps alteration of surname *Elwes*. Few regular variants.

Elye: see **Elijah**

Emanuel Biblical name, from Hebrew '*Immānūēl*, "God (is) with us." Alternate spelling, **Emmanuel**, is not uncommon. Spanish variant, **Manuel**, found mainly in the U.S. Old Testament version of name, **Immanuel**, is now in German use, as for philosopher Immanuel Kant (1724–1804). Diminutives are usually **Man** and **Manny**.

Emil: see **Emile**

Emile French form (properly *Émile*) of Latin name *Aemilius* (which gave **Emily**). German form of name, **Emil**, also occurs.

Emlyn Welsh name, perhaps from Latin name *Aemilius* (which gave **Emily**). No established variants.

Emmanuel: see **Emanuel**

Emrys Welsh form of **Ambrose**. No regular variants.

Enoch Biblical name, from Hebrew *Hānōkh*, perhaps meaning "dedicated." No regular variants.

Ephraim Biblical name, from Hebrew *Ephrayim*, "very fruitful." Diminutive variant, **Effie**, occurs.

Erasmus From Latin form of Greek name *Erasmos*, itself based on *erān*, "to love" or "to long for." Few established variants.

Erastus From Greek name *Erastos*, meaning "dear one" or "beloved." Fairly common variant is **Rastus**.

Eric From Old Norse name *Eyrekr*, comprising *ei*, "ever" or "always," and *ríkr*, "ruler": "ever-ruling." Variant spelling, **Erik**, and diminutive, **Rick**, are used independently.

Erik Independently adopted Swedish variant of **Eric**. Variant diminutive, **Rick**, is in independent use.

Erle: see **Earl**

Ern: see **Ernest**

Ernest From Old German name *Ernust*, corresponding to modern German *Ernst*, meaning "seriousness" or "earnestness," implying "battler to the death." Diminutive variant, **Ernie**, is in independent use, and further diminutive is **Ern**.

Ernie Independently adopted diminutive of **Ernest**. In regular English-speaking use from late nineteenth century. Diminutive variant, **Ern**, is also common.

Errol From Scottish surname, but popularly associated with **Earl**. Variant spelling, **Erroll**, exists, as for jazz pianist Erroll Garner (1921–1977).

Erroll: see **Errol**

Erskine From Scottish surname. Few established variants.

Esau Biblical name, from Hebrew *'Ēsāw*, "hairy." No regular variants.

Esme French name (properly *Esmé*), from Old French *esme* (modern French *aimé*, but also English *esteemed*), "loved" (compare to **Amy** or to female name **Esme**). No regular variants.

Esmond From Old English name *Ēstmund*, comprising *ēst*, "favor" or "grace," and *mund*, "protection": "favored protector." No regular variants.

Ethan Biblical name, from Hebrew *Ēythān*, "firm" or "strong." No established variants.

Ethelbert From Old English name *Æthelbeorht*, comprising *æthele*, "noble," and *beorht*, "bright," giving more recent **Albert**. No regular variants.

Ethelred From Old English name *Æthelrǽd*, comprising *āthele*, "noble," and *rǽd*, "counsel": "noble counsel." No variants.

Eugene From French form of Greek name *Eugenios*, itself meaning "well-born" or "noble." Diminutive variant, **Gene**, is in independent use, especially in the U.S.

Eustace From French form of Greek name *Eustakhios*, comprising *eu-*, "good" or "well," and *stakhys*, "ear of corn": "fruitful." Diminutive variant, **Stacy**, became independent name.

Evan English form of Welsh *Iefan* (**John**). Few established variants, though **Van** could evolve as diminutive.

Evelyn From surname. Compare to female name **Evelyn**. No regular variants.

Everard From Old German name *Everart*, comprising *eber*, "boar," and *hart*, "brave" or "strong": "fierce as a boar." Few established variants.

Everett From surname (itself variant of **Everard**). Variant spelling, **Everitt**, occurs.

Everitt: see **Everett**

Ewan English form of Gaelic name *Eóghan* (**Owen**), but also popularly associated with **Evan**. Variant spelling, **Ewen**, occurs.

Ewart From surname. Few established variants.

Ewen: see **Ewan**

Ezekiel Biblical name, from Hebrew *Yehezqēl*, "God will strengthen." Regular diminutive variant is **Zeke.**

Ezra Biblical name, from Hebrew *'Ezrā*, "help," (i.e., that of God). Few regular variants.

Fabian English form of Latin name *Fabianus*, from Roman clan name *Fabius*, itself probably deriving from *faba*, "bean," implying "one who grows beans." No regular variants.

Feargus: see **Fergus**

Felix Biblical name, from Latin name *Felix*, meaning "lucky" or "happy." No established variants.

Ferd: see **Ferdinand**

Ferdie: see **Ferdinand**

Ferdinand English form of Old German name *Fridenand*, comprising *fridu*, "peace," and *nand*, "bravery": "peace through bravery." Spanish form of name, **Fernando**, has been adopted by some English speakers. Diminutives **Ferd**, **Ferdie**, and **Ferdy** exist.

Ferdy: see **Ferdinand**

Fergie: see **Fergus**

Fergus English form of Gaelic name *Fearghas*, comprising *fear*, "man," and *gus*, "force": "man of force." Regular diminutives are **Fergie** and **Fergy**.

Fergy: see **Fergus**

Fernando: see **Ferdinand**

Festus Biblical name, from Latin name *Festus*, meaning "in holiday mood" or "festal." No regular variants.

Fletcher From surname. No variants.

Florian English form of Latin name *Florianus*, itself from *Florus*, representing *flos*, genitive *floris*, "flower." No established variants.

Floyd From surname, itself variant of **Lloyd**. No regular variants.

Forest: see **Forrest**

Forrest From surname. Occasional variant spelling, **Forest**, exists.

Foster From surname. No regular variants.

Francis English form of late Latin name *Franciscus*, "Frenchman." Regular diminutive variants, **Frank** and **Frankie**, are names in own right.

Frank Originally Germanic name relating to tribe of Franks, who gave name of France. Now usually regarded as independently adopted diminutive of **Francis** or **Franklin**. Diminutive variant, **Frankie**, is in independent use.

Frankie Independently adopted diminutive of **Francis** or **Frank**. Few regular variants.

Franklin From surname. Regular diminutive variant is **Frank**, in independent use.

Fred Independently adopted diminutive of **Frederick**, or (less often), **Alfred**. Regular diminutive, **Freddie**, is name in own right.

Freddie Independently adopted diminutive of **Fred** or **Frederick**. Alternate spelling, **Freddy**, exists.

Freddy: see **Freddie**

Frederic: see **Frederick**

Frederick From Old German name, (modern German is *Friedrich*), comprising *fridu*, "peace," and *rīchi*, "powerful" or "ruler": "peaceful ruler." Alternate spellings include **Frederic** and **Fredric.** Regular diminutives are **Fred** and **Freddie**, both in independent use.

Fritz Diminutive form of German *Friedrich* (**Frederick**). Few, if any, regular variants exist.

Gabby: see **Gabriel**

Gabriel Biblical name, from Hebrew *Gabhrī'ēl*, "my strength is God." Diminutive variant, **Gabby**, occurs.

Gamaliel Biblical name, from Hebrew *Gamlī'ēl*, "my reward is God." No regular variants.

Gareth Welsh name, variant of **Geraint**, though also popularly associated with **Garth**, **Gary**, and even **Gerard**. Few regular variants.

Garfield From surname. Diminutive variants, **Gary** and **Garry**, exist, the former in independent use (and actually different name).

Garry: see **Garfield** and **Gary**

Garth From surname, but often popularly associated with **Gareth**. No regular variants.

Gary From surname, but popularly associated with **Gareth**. Alternate spelling, **Garry**, occurs.

Gavin Scottish form of **Gawain**. Few established variants.

Gawain Welsh name, based on *gwalch*, "hawk." **Gavin** is independently adopted variant of name.

Gayelord: see **Gaylord**

Gaylord From surname, itself distortion of French *gaillard*, "dandy" or "merry fellow." Variant spelling, **Gayelord**, exists.

Gene Independently adopted diminutive of **Eugene**. No regular variants.

Geoff: see **Geoffrey**

Geoffrey From Old German name *Gaufrid*, probably comprising *gauja*, "territory," and *fridu*, "peace," implying "peaceful ruler," but seen by some as variant of **Godfrey**. Variant spelling, **Jeffrey**, is in independent use. Regular diminutive is **Geoff**.

Geordie: see **George**

George English version of (ultimately) Greek name *Georgios*, itself from *geōrgos*, "farmer," (literally, "earth worker"). Regular diminutive variants are **Georgie**, **Georgy**, and **Geordie**. Last of these is Scottish and northern English form.

Georgie: see **George**

Georgy: see **George**

Geraint Welsh name, of uncertain Celtic origin, but probably influenced by Greek *gerōn*, genitive *gerontos*, "Old man." No regular variants.

Gerald English form of Old German name *Gerwald*, comprising *gēr*, "spear," and *waltan*, "to rule": "spear ruler." Associated with **Gerard**, but that is a different name. Regular diminutive variants, **Gerry** and **Jerry**, are both in independent use.

Gerard English form of Old German name *Gerart*, comprising *gēr*, "spear," and *hart*, "strong" or "brave": "brave with the spear." Associated with **Gerard**, but that is a different name. Regular diminutive variants, **Gerry** and **Jerry,** are both in independent use.

Gerry Independently adopted diminutive of **Gerald. Jerry** is alternate spelling in independent use.

Gershom Biblical name, from Hebrew *Gērshōm*, "exile." No regular variants.

Gervaise: see **Gervase**

Gervase English form of late Latin name *Gervasius*, perhaps in turn based either on Greek *gēras*, "old age," or compound of Old German *gēr*, "spear," and *vas*, "servant" or "vassal." Variant spelling, **Gervaise**, exists. Directly related name is **Jarvis**.

Gib: see **Gilbert**

Gideon Biblical name, from Hebrew *Gid'ōn*, "one who cuts down," (i.e., "swordsman"). Few established variants.

Gilbert English form (through French) of Old German name comprising *gisil*, "pledge," and *berht*, "bright" or "famous": "famous pledger." Variant diminutive is usually **Gib.**

Giles English form, through French and much altered, of (ultimately) Greek name *Aigidios*, from *aigidion*, "kid" or "young goat." Reference is to kid leather, used for making shields. Variant spelling, **Gyles**, sometimes found.

Ginger From nickname, usually for person with red hair or fiery temper. Compare to female name **Ginger.** Few regular variants.

Glen: see **Glenn**

Glenn From surname. Compare to female name **Glenn.**

Variant spelling, **Glen**, also occurs, as for country singer Glen Campbell (born 1936).

Glyn Welsh name, from *glyn*, "valley," influenced by **Glenn** and perhaps also by **Gwyn**. Variant spelling, **Glynn**, occurs.

Glynn: see **Glyn**

Godfrey English form of Old German name *Godafrid*, from *god*, "god," and *fridu*, "peace": "peace god." Associated with **Geoffrey**, but that is a different name. Few regular variants.

Godwin From Old English name *Godwine*, comprising *god*, "god," and *wine*, "friend": "God (is) friend." No established variants.

Gorden: see **Gordon**

Gordon From Scottish surname. Occasional spelling variant is **Gorden**.

Graeme: see **Graham**

Graham From Scottish surname. Variant spelling, **Graeme**, is not uncommon in Scotland.

Grant From Scottish surname. No regular variants.

Granville From surname. Variant, **Grenville**, exists.

Greg: see **Gregory**

Gregg: see **Gregory**

Gregory English form of Greek name *Gregōrios*, itself from *gregōrein*, "to watch": "watchful" or "vigilant." Regular diminutive variant is **Greg** (also **Gregg** or **Greig** in Scotland).

Greig: see **Gregory**

Grenville: see **Granville**

Greville From surname. No regular variants.

Griff: see **Griffith**

Griffith English form of Welsh name *Gruffudd*, second part of which means "lord" or "chief." Regular diminutive variant is **Griff.**

Gus Independently adopted diminutive of **Angus, Augustus,** or **Gustav.** Few regular variants.

Gustav Scandinavian name, originally *Götstaf,* perhaps comprising *got,* "god," and *stafr,* "staff": "staff of the gods." Variant Latin form, **Gustavus,** also occurs. Diminutive is **Gus.**

Gustavus: see **Gustav**

Guy English form (through French) of Old German name, perhaps itself derived from *wīt,* "wide," or *witu,* "wood." No established variants.

Gwyn Welsh name, originally nickname, from *gwyn,* "white," "fair," or "blessed," (compare to **Gwendolen**). No regular variants.

Gyles: see **Giles**

Habakkuk Biblical name, from Hebrew *Habaqqūq*, "embrace." No regular variants.

Hal Independently adopted diminutive of **Harry** or **Henry**. No established variants.

Hamilton From Scottish surname. Few regular variants.

Hamish English form of Gaelic name *Sheumais*, vocative of *Seumas* (**James**). No established variants.

Hamlet English form (through French diminutive) of Old German name *Heimo*, from *heim*, "house" or "home" (so etymologically equated with modern English "hamlet"). Related name, **Hammond**, is in independent use.

Hammond From surname (itself from Old German name that gave **Hamlet**). No established variants.

Hank Originally form of *Hankin*, diminutive of *Han* (form of **John**), but now generally regarded as independently adopted diminutive of **Henry**. No regular variants.

Hannibal From Latin name, itself from Phoenician name comprising *hann*, "grace" (indirectly related to **Hannah**), and *Baal* (name of god): "grace of Baal." No regular variants.

Hans German form of **John**. No regular variants.

Hardy From surname, perhaps with influence from standard word "hardy" (also represented in familiar names such as **Bernard** and **Richard**). No regular variants.

Harlan From surname. No regular variants.

Harley From surname. Few established variants.

Harold From Old English name *Hereweald*, comprising *here*, "army," and *wealdan*, "to rule": "army ruler." Spelling is influenced by Scandinavian equivalent name, *Haraldr*. No regular variants, though **Walter** is related name.

Harrison From surname. Diminutive variant, **Harry**, is really of a different origin.

Harry Independently adopted diminutive of **Henry**. Diminutive, **Hal**, is in independent use.

Hartley From surname. No regular variants.

Harvey From surname. No regular variants.

Havelock From surname. No established variants.

Haydn From surname of Austrian composer Joseph Haydn. No regular variants.

Heckie: see **Hector**

Hector From Greek name *Hektōr*, probably based on *ekhein*, "to hold" or "to resist." Scottish diminutive variant, **Heckie**, exists.

Henry English form of Old German name *Heimerich*, comprising *heim*, "house" or "home," and *rīchi*, "ruler" or "owner": "home ruler" or "house owner" (i.e., "lord of the manor"). Regular diminutives, **Hal**, **Hank**, and **Harry**, are in independent use, and **Bunny** is sometimes also found.

Herb Independently adopted diminutive of **Herbert**. Variant diminutive, **Herbie**, is also in independent use.

Herbert From Old English name *Herebeorht*, comprising *here*, "army," and *beorht*, "bright" or "famous": "famous army." (This in turn is a variant of Old German name of identical meaning.) Regular diminutive variants are **Herb** and **Herbie**, in independent use.

Herbie Independently adopted diminutive of **Herbert** or **Herb**. Few established variants.

Hercules Latin form of Greek name *Hēraklēs*, traditionally derived from *Hēra* (queen of Olympian gods), and *kleos*, "glory": "glory of Hera." No regular variants.

Herman English form of Old German name *Hariman*, comprising *hari*, "army," and *man*, "man": "army man" or "warrior." Less common spelling variant, **Hermann**, also found.

Hermann: see **Herman**

Hezekiah Biblical name, from Hebrew *Hizqīyāh*, "my strength is Yah" (i.e., Jehovah). No established variants.

Hilary English form of Latin name *Hilarius*, itself from *hilaris*, "cheerful," (hence, English word, "hilarious"). Compare to female name **Hilary**. Variant spelling, **Hillary**, occurs.

Hillary: see **Hilary**

Hiram Biblical name, from Hebrew *Hīrām*, perhaps shortened form of *Ahīrām*, "my brother is exalted." Variant spelling, **Hyram**, exists.

Homer Either from Greek name *Homēros*, perhaps meaning "hostage," or from surname. No regular variants.

Horace English form of Roman clan name *Horatius*, perhaps itself related to Latin *hora*, "time" or "hour." **Horatio** is directly related name.

Horatio Independently adopted variant form of **Horace**, influenced by Latin *Horatius* and Italian *Orazio*. Few regular variants.

Howard From surname. Few established variants, although diminutive, **Howie**, occurs.

Howell Either from surname or as English form of Welsh name, **Hywel**. No regular variants.

Howie: see **Howard**

Hubert English form of Old German name *Hugibert*, comprising *hug*, "heart" or "mind" (as for **Hugh**), and *beraht*, "bright" or "shining": "bright spirit." Few established variants.

Hugh English form of Germanic name, based on *hug*, "heart" or "mind" (as for **Hubert**). Diminutive variant, **Hughie**, is in independent use, as are the Latin revival, **Hugo**, and the Welsh form, **Huw**.

Hughie Independently adopted diminutive of **Hugh**. Few regular variants.

Hugo English adoption of Latin form of **Hugh**. Few established variants.

Hum: see **Humbert**

Humbert English form of Old German (later Old English)

name comprising *hun*, "Hun," and *beraht*, "bright" or
"famous": "famous Hun." Few established variants, although
diminutive, **Hum**, exists.

Humph: see **Humphrey**

Humphrey English form of Old German (later Old English)
name *Hunfred*, comprising *hun*, "Hun," and *fridu*, "peace":
"peaceful Hun." Variant spelling, **Humphry**, occurs. Regular
diminutive is **Humph**.

Humphry: see **Humphrey**

Huw Welsh form of **Hugh**. No regular variants.

Hyram: see **Hiram**

Hywel Welsh name, meaning "conspicuous" (and giving
English form **Howell**). No regular variants.

Iain Gaelic form of **Ian**. No regular variants.

Ian Scottish version of **John**. Gaelic variant, **Iain**, is in independent use.

Ichabod Biblical name, from Hebrew *Ī-khābhōdh*, "where is the glory?" (interpreted as "without glory"). No variants noted.

Idris Welsh name, comprising *iud*, "lord," and *rīs*, "ardent": "impulsive ruler." No established variants.

Ifor Welsh name, of uncertain origin but traditionally derived from *iôr*, "lord." Now associated with **Ivor**, but that name has a different origin. No established variants.

Ignatius From Late Latin name, itself from Roman clan name *Egnatius*, of uncertain origin, but altered by association with *ignis*, "fire." No established variants.

Igor Russian name, from Scandinavian *Ingvarr*, comprising *Ing*, "Ing" (Norse fertility god), and *varr*, "careful" or "attentive": "cared for by Ing." No established variants.

Ike: see **Isaac**

Illtud: see **Illtyd**

Illtyd Welsh name, comprising *il*, "multitude," and *tud*, "land": "land of the people." Alternate spelling, **Illtud**, exists.

Immanuel Independently adopted variant of **Emanuel**. Regular diminutive variant is **Manny**.

Inigo English form of Spanish name *Íñigo* (**Ignatius**). No established variants.

Iolo Welsh name, independently adopted diminutive of **Iorwerth**, though popularly associated with **Julius**. No regular variants.

Iorwerth Welsh name, comprising *iôr*, "lord" and *berth*, "beautiful": "handsome lord." No regular variants.

Ira Biblical name, from Hebrew *'Īrā*, "watchful." Few established variants.

Irving From Scottish surname. Few established variants.

Irwin From surname, although sometimes associated with **Irving**. Few regular variants.

Isaac Biblical name, from Hebrew *Yitschāq*, "he will laugh." Alternate spelling, **Izaak**, exists, as do others. Israeli prime minister Yitzhak Shamir (born 1915) and Israeli violinist Itzhak Perlman (born 1945) have Hebrew forms of name. Regular diminutives are **Ike** and **Zak**.

Isaiah Biblical name, from Hebrew *Yĕsha'yāh*, "salvation of Yah" (i.e., Jehovah). Few established variants.

Ishmael Biblical name, from Hebrew *Yishmā'ēl*, "God will hearken." No established variants.

Isidore English form of Greek name *Isidōros*, comprising *Isis* (Egyptian goddess) and *dōron*, "gift": "gift of Isis." Originally regarded as Christian version of Jewish name, **Isaiah**. No regular variants, although diminutive, **Izzy**, has been noted.

Israel Biblical name, from Hebrew *Yisrā'ēl*, comprising *sārāh*, "to struggle," and *ēl*, "God": "he who struggles with

God" or "rival against God." Few established variants, although diminutives, **Issy** and **Izzy**, occur.

Issy: see **Israel**

Ivan Russian form of **John**. Few established variants, though **Van** can evolve as independently adopted diminutive.

Ivor English form of Scandinavian name, *Ivarr*, comprising *ýr*, "yew," and *arr*, "warrior": "bowman" (bows were made of yew). Now associated with **Ifor**, though that is a different name. No regular variants.

Izaak: see **Isaac**

Izzy: see **Isidore** and **Israel**

Jabez Biblical name, from Hebrew *Ya'bēts*, "he causes sorrow." No established variants.

Jack Independently adopted diminutive of **John**, through Middle English *Jankin* (later, *Jackin*), where *-kin* is a diminutive suffix. Variant, **Jake**, and diminutive, **Jackie**, are in independent use.

Jackie Independently adopted diminutive of **Jack** or **John**. Compare to female name **Jackie**. Spelling variant, **Jacky**, exists.

Jackson From surname. Diminutive variants as for **Jack** can occur.

Jacky: see **Jackie**

Jacob Biblical name, from Hebrew *Ya'akub-'ēl*, "May God protect," but traditionally derived from *āqēb*, "heel," or closely related word *āqāb*, "to usurp," together implying a person who follows on the heels of another and supplants him. See also **James**. **Jake** is sometimes regarded as diminutive in independent use.

Jake Variant of **Jack** in independent use, also sometimes regarded as diminutive of **Jacob**. No regular variants.

James Biblical name, from late Latin name *Jacomus*, variant of *Jacobus* (**Jacob**). Regular diminutive variants, **Jim** and **Jamie** (latter preferred Scottish form), are in independent use.

Jamie Independently adopted diminutive of **James**. Compare to female name, **Jamie**. No established variants.

Japheth Biblical name, from Hebrew *Yepheth*, "enlargement" or "expansion." No regular variants.

Jared Biblical name, from Hebrew *Yeredh*, "descended." No established variants.

Jarvis From surname, itself a form of **Gervase**. Variant spelling, **Jervis**, occasionally occurs.

Jason English form of Greek name *Iasōn*, itself probably based on *iasthai*, "to heal." Also biblical name, probably as classical form of **Joshuah**. No regular variants.

Jasper Perhaps ultimately from Persian word meaning "treasurer." Not from "jasper" (gemstone). Dutch variant, **Caspar**, is also in English-speaking use.

Jay Either from surname or as independently adopted diminutive formed from name beginning *J-*, such as **James**. Not from the bird, which was from Roman name *Gaius* (compare to **Robin**). Compare to female name **Jay**. No established variants.

Jed Independently adopted diminutive of **Jedidiah** or **Jacob**. Few regular variants.

Jedidiah Biblical name, from Hebrew *Jedīd'yāh*, "friend of Yah" (i.e., Jehovah), otherwise "befriended by God." Regular diminutive variant is **Jed**, in independent use.

Jeff Independently adopted diminutive of **Jeffrey**, or, less often, **Jefferson**. No regular variants.

Jefferson From surname. Regular diminutive is **Jeff**, in independent use.

Jeffrey Independently adopted variant of **Geoffrey**. Regular diminutive, **Jeff**, is in independent use.

Jem Originally diminutive form of **James**, but now regarded as independently adopted diminutive of **Jeremy**. Diminutive variant, **Jemmy**, exists.

Jemmy: see **Jem**

Jephtha: see **Jephthah**

Jephthah Biblical name, from Hebrew *Yiphtah*, "he (i.e., God) opens." No established variants, though **Jephtha** and **Jeptha** sometimes occur.

Jeremiah Biblical name, from Hebrew *Yirměyāh*, "exalted by Yah" (i.e. Jehovah). Regular diminutive variant is **Jerry**, adopted in own right.

Jeremy English form of **Jeremiah**. Sometimes associated with **Jerome**, but that is a different name. Regular diminutive variant, **Jerry**, is independent use.

Jerome English form of Greek name *Hieronymos*, comprising *hieros*, "holy," and *onoma*, "name": "one who bears a holy name." Associated with **Jeremy**, but that is a name of different origin. Regular diminutive, **Jerry**, is in independent use.

Jerry Either independently adopted diminutive of **Jeremy**, **Jeremiah**, or **Jerome**, or spelling variant of **Gerry**. No regular variants.

Jervis: see **Jarvis**

Jess: see **Jesse**

Jesse Biblical name, from Hebrew *Yīshay*, meaning either

"Jehovah exists" or "gift of Jehovah." Pronunciation is normally as female version **Jessie**, but sometimes as **Jess**. Regular diminutive is **Jess**.

Jethro Biblical name, from Hebrew *Yitrŏ,* "excellence." No established variants.

Jim Independently adopted diminutive of **James**. Regular diminutive variant is **Jimmy**, in independent use.

Jimi: see **Jimmy**

Jimmie: see **Jimmy**

Jimmy Independently adopted diminutive of **James** and its own diminutive, **Jim**. Spelling variants, **Jimmie** and **Jimi**, exist, latter as for rock musician Jimi Hendrix (1942–1970).

Jo Independently adopted diminutive of **Joseph** or variant spelling of **Joe**. No regular variants.

Joab Biblical name, from Hebrew *Yō'ābh,* "Jehovah is father." No established variants.

Joachim Biblical name, from Hebrew *Yehoyaqim,* "Jehovah will establish." No regular variants.

Job Biblical name, from Hebrew *Iyyōbh,* "persecuted." Few established variants.

Jocelin: see **Jocelyn**

Jocelyn From surname, itself from personal name *Joscelin,* introduced to England by Normans. Compare to female name **Jocelyn**. Many spelling variants include, **Jocelin**, **Joscelyn**, and **Josslyn**. Diminutive, **Joss**, is in independent use.

Jodi: see **Jody**

Jody Apparently independently adopted diminutive of names such as **George, Jude,** or elaborated form of **Joe.** Compare to female name **Jody.** Spelling variant is **Jodi.**

Joe Independently adopted diminutive of **Joseph** or, less often, **John** or **Joshua.** Variant diminutives in independent use are **Jo** and **Joey.**

Joel Biblical name, from Hebrew *Yō'ēl*, "Yah is god" (i.e., Yahweh, or Jehovah, is only true god). No regular variants.

Joey Independently adopted diminutive of **Joseph, Joshua,** or **Joe.** No regular variants.

John Biblical name, from Hebrew *Yōhānān*, "Yah has been gracious" (Yah being Jehovah, or God). Spelling variant, **Jon,** is name in own right. Regular diminutives in independent use include **Jack, Johnny,** and **Hank.** Non-English forms of name in English-speaking use include **Hans, Ian, Ivan, Juan,** and **Sean.**

Johnathan: see **Jonathan**

Johnnie: see **Johnny**

Johnny Independently adopted diminutive of **John.** Alternate spelling, **Johnnie,** is also common, as for pop singer Johnnie Ray (1927–1990).

Jolly: see **Jolyon**

Jolyon Independently adopted northern English form of **Julian.** Diminutive variant, **Jolly,** exists.

Jon Independently adopted diminutive of **Jonathan** or spelling variant of **John.** Few established variants.

Jonah Biblical name, from Hebrew *Yōnāh*, "dove." Variant, **Jonas**, is in independent use.

Jonas English form of Greek name *Iōnas* (**Jonah**). Diminutive variant, **Joney**, exists.

Jonathan Biblical name, from Hebrew *Yěhōnāthān*, "Yah (i.e., Jehovah) has given" (compare to **Nathan** and **Nathaniel**). Associated with **John**, but that name has a different origin. Spelling variant, **Jonathon**, occurs, as does **Johnathan**, by association with John. Regular diminutive, in independent use, is **Jon**.

Jonathon: see **Jonathan**

Joney: see **Jonas**

Jools: see **Jules** and **Julian**

Joscelyn: see **Jocelyn**

Joseph Biblical name, from Hebrew *Yōsēph*, "(God) may add (another son)." Regular diminutive variants, **Joe** and **Joey**, are in independent use.

Josh Independently adopted diminutive of **Joshua** or **Josiah**. No established variants.

Joshua Biblical name, from Hebrew *Yěhōshū'a*, "Yah (i.e., Jehovah) saves." Diminutive variants include **Joe** and **Josh**, both in independent use.

Josiah Biblical name, from Hebrew *Yōshīyāh*, "Yah supports" (Yah being Jehovah). Diminutive variant, **Josh**, is in independent use.

Joss Independently adopted diminutive of **Jocelyn**. No regular variants.

Josslyn: see **Jocelyn**

Jotham Biblical name, from Hebrew *Yōthām*, "Yah (i.e., Jehovah) is perfect." No regular variants.

Juan Spanish form of **John**. No regular variants.

Jubal Biblical name, from Hebrew *Jōbel*, "horn" or "trumpet" (giving English word "jubilee"). No established variants.

Judah Biblical name, from Hebrew *Yĕhūdhāh*, "he who is praised." **Judas** and **Jude** are directly related names.

Judas Biblical name, Greek form of **Judah**. **Judah** and **Jude** are directly related names.

Jude Biblical name, English shortened form of **Judas**. No established variants.

Jules Either French form of **Julius** or independently adopted diminutive of **Julian**. Spelling variant **Jools** occurs.

Julian English form of Late Latin name *Julianus*, itself a derivative of **Julius**. **Jolyon** is variant form of name, while **Jules** is regular diminutive, in independent use. Alternate spelling, **Julyan**, and diminutive, **Jools**, also occur.

Julius Roman clan name, of uncertain origin. Bearers of name claimed descent from *Iulus*, son of Aeneas. **Jules** is directly related name.

Julyan: see **Julian**

Junior From nickname for young person, or family designation "Jr." Perhaps sometimes variant of name such as **Julian**. Few established variants.

Justie: see **Justin**

Justin English form of Latin name *Justinus*, derivative of **Justus**. **Justie** and **Justy** are sometimes diminutive variants.

Justus Latin name, meaning "fair" or "just." No established variants.

Justy: see **Justin**

Kane English form of Gaelic name *Cathán*, itself diminutive form of Irish *cath*, "battle." No regular variants.

Karel: see **Carol**

Karl: see **Carl**

Kasey: see **Casey**

Kaspar: see **Caspar**

Kasper: see **Caspar**

Kay Probably English form of Roman name *Gaius*, itself of uncertain origin. Compare to female name **Kay**. Too rare to have regular variants.

Keir From Scottish surname. No established variants.

Keith From Scottish surname. No regular variants.

Ken Independently adopted diminutive of **Kenneth**, or of some other name beginning *Ken-*, such as **Kendal**, **Kenelm**, or **Kennedy**. Diminutive variant, **Kenny**, is in independent use.

Kendal From surname. Variant spelling, **Kendall**, also found.

Kendall: see **Kendal**

Kendrick From Welsh or Scottish surname. Alternate spelling, **Kenrick**, exists.

Kenelm From Old English name *Cenelm*, comprising *cēne*, "bold" or "keen," and *helm*, "helmet" or "protection": "bold defender." No regular variants.

Kenith: see **Kenneth**

Kennedy From Irish surname. No regular variants, although **Ken** and **Kenny** are logical developments.

Kenneth English form of two Gaelic names: *Cinead*, perhaps meaning "born of fire," and *Cainneach*, meaning "handsome." Variant spellings are **Kennith** and **Kenith**. Regular diminutives in independent use are **Ken** and **Kenny**.

Kennith: see **Kenneth**

Kenny Independently adopted diminutive of **Kenneth**. Alternate diminutive, **Ken,** is also in independent use.

Kenrick: see **Kendrick**

Kent From surname. No regular variants.

Kermit English form of Gaelic surname *Mac Dhiarmaid* (which itself gave **Dermot**). No established variants.

Kerrie: see **Kerry**

Kerry From surname. Compare to female name **Kerry**. Variant spelling, **Kerrie,** sometimes found.

Kev: see **Kevin**

Kevan: see **Kevin**

Kevin English form of Gaelic name *Caoimhín*, itself based on Irish *caomh*, "gentle," "fair," or "friend." Alternate spelling, **Kevan**, occurs, while usual diminutive is **Kev**.

Kid From nickname for young or distinctive person. No regular variants.

Kieran English form of Gaelic name *Ciarán*, itself diminutive of Irish *ciar*, "black," so "little black-haired one." Alternate spelling, **Kieron**, exists.

Kieron: see **Kieran**

Kim Independently adopted diminutive of **Kimberley**. Compare to female name **Kim**. No regular variants.

Kimberley From name of a South African town. Variant spelling, **Kimberly**, also occurs.

Kimberly: see **Kimberley**

King From royal title (compare to **Duke, Earl,** and **Leroy**). Few established variants.

Kingsley From surname. No regular variants.

Kirk From Scottish surname. Variant spelling, **Kirke**, exists.

Kirke: see **Kirk**

Kit Independently adopted diminutive of **Christopher**. No regular variants.

Kurt Independently adopted diminutive of German name *Konrad* (**Conrad**). Variant spelling, **Curt**, exists.

Kyle From Scottish surname. Compare to female name **Kyle**. Few regular variants.

Laban Biblical name, from Hebrew *Lābhān*, "white." (Compare to Lebanon, so named for its snowy mountain peaks.) No regular variants.

Lachie: see **Lachlan**

Lachlan English form of Scottish name *Lachlann*, earlier *Lochlann*, said to refer to immigrant from Norway, "land of lochs." Scottish diminutive variant, **Lachie**, exists, but usually is spelled **Lockie** in Canada.

Lambert From Old German name, comprising *lant*, "land" or "territory," and *beraht*, "bright" or "famous": "famous landowner." Few established variants, although **Bert** is a good candidate for diminutive.

Lance Either independently adopted diminutive of **Lancelot**, or from Old German name based on *lant*, "land" (as for **Lambert**), or adoption of French word *lance*, "lance" (the weapon), so meaning "warrior." No regular variants.

Lancelot Of doubtful origin, but not connected with "lance," despite knightly connotations. Perhaps through Old French *l'ancelle* from Latin *ancillus*, "servant," or from some earlier Celtic source. Alternate spelling, **Launcelot**, is found widely in literature, as is diminutive, **Launce**. **Lance** is still active in independent use.

Larry Independently adopted diminutive of **Laurence** or **Lawrence**. Diminutive variant, **Laz**, now occurs.

Launce: see **Lancelot**

Launcelot: see **Lancelot**

Laurence English form (through French) of Latin name *Laurentius*, "man from Laurentum" (town in Latium whose own name is associated with Latin *laurus*, "laurel," with figurative sense "triumph" or "victory"). Alternate spelling, **Lawrence**, is usually in distinct use. Regular diminutive in independent use is **Larry**, while **Laurie** is also common.

Laurie: see **Laurence**

Lawrence English form of (French-spelled) **Laurence**. Regular diminutive variant in independent use is **Larry**, while **Lawrie** is also found.

Lawrie: see **Lawrence**

Laz: see **Larry**

Lazarus Biblical name, from Latinized version of Hebrew *El'āzār*, "God has helped" (same name as biblical Eleazar). No established variants.

Lea: see **Lee**

Leander Latin form of Greek name *Leandros*, comprising *leōn*, "lion," and *anēr*, genitive *andros*, "man": so "lion man" or "strong and brave man." No established variants.

Lee From surname. Compare to female name **Lee**. Variant spellings, **Lea** and **Leigh**, exist.

Leigh: see **Lee**

Lemie: see **Lemmy**

Lemmie: see **Lemmy**

Lemmy Independently adopted diminutive of **Lemuel**. No regular variants, although **Lemie** and **Lemmie** have been noted.

Lemuel Biblical name, from Hebrew *Lĕmū'ēl*, "devoted to God." Diminutive variant, **Lemmy**, is in independent use.

Len Independently adopted diminutive of **Leonard**. Diminutive variant, **Lennie**, is in independent use.

Lennard: see **Leonard**

Lennie Independently adopted diminutive of **Leonard** or **Len**. Alternate spelling, **Lenny**, exists, as for comedian Lenny Bruce (1926–1966).

Lennox From Scottish surname and earldom. Variant spelling, **Lenox**, exists.

Lenny: see **Lennie**

Lenox: see **Lennox**

Leo From Late Latin name, meaning "lion." No regular variants, but **Leon** is a directly related name.

Leon Ultimately from Greek *leōn* or Latin *leo*, genitive *leonis*, "lion." No regular variants.

Leonard From French form of Old German name comprising *lewo*, "lion," and *hart*, "strong" or "hard": "strong as a lion." Alternate spelling, **Lennard**, occurs. Regular diminutives are **Len** and **Lennie**, in independent use.

Lennard: see **Leonard**

Leopold English form of Old German name *Liutpold*, comprising *liut*, "people" or "race," and *bald*, "bold" or "brave": "of a brave people." Few regular variants.

LeRoi: see **Leroy**

Leroy From Old French *le roy,* "the king," originally nickname (compare to **King**). Variant spellings, **LeRoy** and **LeRoi**, are fairly common.

LeRoy: see **Leroy**

Les Independently adopted diminutive of **Leslie** or **Lester.** No established variants.

Leslie From Scottish surname. Compare to female name **Lesley.** Regular diminutive, **Les**, is in independent use.

Lester From surname. Few established variants.

Levi Biblical name, from Hebrew *Lēwī,* "associated" or "attached." Variant spelling, **Levy,** also increasingly found.

Levy: see **Levi**

Lew: see **Lewis**

Lewis English form of French name **Louis.** Regular diminutive variant is **Lew.**

Lex Independently adopted diminutive of **Alexander,** perhaps modeled on **Rex.** Diminutive variant, **Lexy,** occurs. Also see **Alex.**

Lexy: see **Lex**

Liam Independently adopted Irish diminutive of **William.** No established variants.

Lincoln From surname. Few established variants.

Lindsay From Scottish surname. Compare to female name **Lindsay.** Spelling variant, **Lindsey,** exists.

Lindsey: see **Lindsay**

Linford From surname. No regular variants.

Linus Biblical name, from Greek name *Linos*, perhaps from *lineos*, "flaxen": "flaxen-haired" or "fair-haired." No regular variants.

Lionel From French *Lionel*, diminutive of **Leon**. Few established variants, although **Leo** is a directly related name.

Llew: see **Llewellyn**

Llewellyn Welsh name, originally *Llywelyn*, popularly derived from *llyw*, "leader," and *eilun*, "likeness," with modern form influenced by *llew*, "lion," but actually going back to Old Celtic name of uncertain meaning. Regular diminutive variant is **Lynn**, in independent use. **Llew** is also common.

Lloyd From Welsh surname. **Floyd** is directly related name.

Lockie: see **Lachlan**

Logan From Scottish surname. No regular variants.

Lon: see **Lonnie**

Lonnie Either independently adopted diminutive of **Alonso** or variant of **Lennie** influenced by names such as **Don** and **Ron**. Alternate spelling, **Lonny**, exists, with diminutive **Lon**, as for actor Lon Chaney (1883–1930), whose original first name was Alonzo.

Lonny: see **Lonnie**

Lorenzo Italian equivalent of **Laurence**. No regular variants.

Lou Independently adopted diminutive of **Louis**. No established variants.

Louis French form of Old German name *Hlutwig* (modern *Ludwig*), comprising *hlūt*, "famous," and *wig*, "battle": so "famous in battle." Normally retains French pronunciation (no sounded -*s*). Directly related names are **Clovis**, **Lewis** (English form), and **Ludovic**. Regular diminutive is **Lou**, in independent use.

Lucas Either English adoption of Latin name *Lucas* (**Luke**) or from surname. No established variants.

Lucian English form of French *Lucien*, Italian *Luciano*, and the like, themselves from Latin name *Lucianus*, derivative of **Lucius**. No regular variants, although **Luciano** itself occasionally found in English-speaking use.

Luciano: see **Lucian**

Lucius Biblical name, identical in Latin, and probably from *lux*, genitive *lucis*, "light." Variant diminutive, **Lucky**, is sometimes in independent use.

Lucky Either from nickname, with obvious meaning, or as independently adopted diminutive of **Lucius** or **Luke**. No regular variants.

Ludo: see **Ludovic**

Ludovic Either English form of Latin name *Ludovicus*, representing Old German name *Hlutwig* (**Louis**), or English form of Gaelic name *Maol Dòmhnaich*, "devotee of the Lord." Variant spelling, **Ludovick**, exists, while regular diminutive is **Ludo**.

Ludovick: see **Ludovic**

Luke Biblical name, from Greek *Loukas*, "man from Lucania" (region on the west coast of southern Italy). **Lucas**

is a directly related name, and diminutive, **Lucky**, sometimes occurs in independent use.

Luther From German surname. No regular variants.

Lyn: see **Lynn**

Lyndon From surname. Diminutive variant, **Lynn**, is in independent use.

Lynn Independently adopted diminutive of **Llewelyn** or **Lyndon**. Compare to female name **Lynn**. Variant spellings **Lyn** and **Lynne** also exist.

Lynne: see **Lynn**

Magnus From identical Latin byname, meaning "great." No regular variants.

Mahomet: see **Muhammad**

Mal Independently adopted diminutive of **Malcolm** or **Maldwyn**. No established variants.

Malachi Biblical name, from Hebrew *Malākhī*, "my messenger." No regular variants.

Malc: see **Malcolm**

Malcolm English form of Gaelic name *Mael Coluim*, "devotee of (St.) Columba." Diminutive variants, **Mal** (in independent use), and **Malc**, exist.

Man: see **Emanuel**

Manasseh Biblical name, from Hebrew *Mĕnasseh*, "causing to forget." Variant form, **Manasses**, exists.

Manasses: see **Manasseh**

Manfred From Old German name comprising *man*, "man," or *magin*, "strength," and *fridu*, "peace": "man of peace" or "strong man." No regular variants.

Manley From surname, suggesting "manly." No regular variants.

Manny: see **Emanuel** and **Immanuel**

Manuel Spanish form of **Emanuel**. No established variants.

Marc Independently adopted French spelling variant of **Mark**. No regular variants.

Marcel French name, from Latin *Marcellus*, diminutive of **Marcus**. Few established variants.

Marcus Latin name, equivalent of **Mark**, traditionally (but probably wrongly) associated with *Mars*, Roman god of war. Few regular variants.

Marion English form of Latin name *Marianus*, derivative of **Marius**. Compare to female name **Marion**. No regular variants.

Marius Latin name, itself Roman clan name, perhaps derived from *Mars*, Roman god of war, or from *mas*, genitive *maris*, "male" or "manly" (with which Mars has in turn been associated). No established variants.

Mark Biblical name, English form of Latin name **Marcus**. Few established variants or regular diminutives, although **Markie** sometimes occurs.

Markie: see **Mark**

Marlin Apparently alteration (perhaps through French) of **Merlin**. No established variants.

Marlon Perhaps derivative of French name **Marc**, with French diminutive suffix *-lon*, or alteration of **Marion** or **Merlin** (or even blend of these). No regular variants.

Marmaduke Of uncertain origin, although perhaps from Celtic name *Mael Maedóc*, "devotee of Maedóc," latter being name of various Irish saints. Regular diminutive variant is **Duke**, in independent use (normally as "title" name).

Marshall From surname, with suggestion of "marshal." No established variants.

Martin English form of Latin name *Martinus*, itself probably from *Mars*, genitive *Martis*, Roman god of war. Popularly associated by some with names of birds, like **Jay** and **Robin**. Variant spelling, **Martyn**, exists, while regular diminutive, **Marty**, is in independent use.

Marty Independently adopted diminutive of **Martin**. No regular variants.

Martyn: see **Martin**

Marvin From surname, itself from form of **Mervyn**. No regular variants.

Mathias: see **Matthias**

Matt Independently adopted diminutive of **Matthew**. Diminutive, **Mattie**, also occurs.

Matthew Biblical name, from Hebrew *Mattathiāh*, "gift of God." **Matthias** is directly related name. Diminutive, **Matt**, is in independent use (compare to female name **Mattie**).

Matthias Biblical name, Aramaic variant of Hebrew original that gave **Matthew**. Variant spelling, **Mathias**, exists, as for Mathias Bede, father of Adam in George Eliot novel *Adam Bede* (1859).

Mattie: see **Matt**

Maurice English (through French) version of late Latin name *Mauricius*, derivative of *Maurus*, itself meaning "Moor," i.e., "dark-skinned." Diminutive variant, **Mo**, exists.

Max Independently adopted diminutive of **Maximilian** or

Maxwell. No regular variants, although diminutives, **Maxey** and **Maxie**, exist.

Maxey: see **Max**

Maxie: see **Max**

Maximilian From Latin name *Maximilianus*, diminutive of *Maximus*, "greatest." Regular diminutive variant, **Max**, is in independent use.

Maxwell From Scottish surname. Regular diminutive, **Max**, is used independently.

Mel Independently adopted diminutive of **Melvin** or **Melville**. No regular variants.

Melville From Scottish surname. Regular diminutive, **Mel**, is in independent use.

Melvin From Scottish surname. Variant spelling, **Melvyn**, is in distinctive use.

Melvyn Independently adopted variant of **Melvin**. Variant diminutive, **Mel**, is used independently.

Meredith English form of Welsh name *Maredudd*, later *Meredudd*, perhaps blend of *mawredd*, "greatness," and *iudd*, "chief": "great chief." Compare to female name **Meredith**. Diminutive variant, **Merry**, is normally adopted for female, not male use, but can occur.

Merle Perhaps form of surname Merrill, or adoption of female name **Merle**. Few regular variants.

Merlin English form of Welsh name *Myrddin*, probably comprising Old Celtic words meaning respectively, "sea" (modern Welsh *môr*), and "fort" (modern Welsh *dinas*): "holder of sea fort." Alternate spelling, **Merlyn**, exists.

Merlyn: see **Merlin**

Merv: see **Mervyn**

Mervin: see **Mervyn**

Mervyn English form of Welsh name *Merfyn*, probably comprising Old Celtic words meaning respectively, "sea" (modern Welsh *môr*), and "great" (as in modern Welsh *mynydd*, "mountain"): loosely, "sea ruler." Popularly associated with **Marvin**. Variant spelling, **Mervin**, occurs. Usual diminutive is **Merv**.

Micah Biblical name, from Hebrew *Mikhāh*, "who is like Yah?" (i.e., Jehovah), so equivalent of **Michael**. No regular variants.

Michael Biblical name, from Hebrew *Mīkha'ēl*, "who is like God?" so equivalent of **Micah**. Diminutive variants, **Mick**, **Micky**, and **Mike**, are in independent use.

Mick Independently adopted diminutive of **Michael**. **Mickey** is directly related variant.

Mickey Independently adopted diminutive of **Michael**, **Mike**, or **Mick**. Variant spellings, **Mickie** and **Micky**, exist.

Mickie: see **Mickey**

Micky: see **Mickey**

Mike Independently adopted diminutive of **Michael**. **Mick** is directly related name. Diminutive is **Mikey**.

Mikey: see **Mike**

Miles Perhaps English form of Latin name **Milo**, itself possibly connected with Slavonic root word *mil*, "dear," but usually associated with Latin *miles*, "soldier," and hence, with **Michael** (similar name with similar "military" sense). Variant spelling, **Myles**, exists, as for English colonist, Pilgrim Fathers military leader, Myles Standish (1584–1656).

Milo English adoption of Latin name that perhaps gave **Miles**. No regular variants.

Milt: see **Milton**

Milton From surname. Diminutive variant, **Milt**, occurs, as for jazz musician Milt Buckner (1915–1977).

Mitch: see **Mitchell**

Mitchell From surname, itself a form of **Michael**. Regular diminutive variant is **Mitch**.

Mo: see **Maurice** and **Moses**

Montague From surname. Regular diminutive variant is **Monty**.

Montgomery From surname. Regular diminutive variant is **Monty**.

Monty: see **Montague** and **Montgomery**

Mordecai Biblical name, probably of Persian origin meaning "devotee of Marduk" (chief Babylonian god). Diminutive variants, **Mordy** and **Morty**, exist.

Mordy: see **Mordecai**

Morgan English form of Welsh name *Morcant*, of uncertain origin, but popularly derived from *môr*, "sea," and *cant*, "circle," or "edge," as if for person born by or who defends a sea's edge. Compare to female name **Morgan.** No established variants.

Morris Independently adopted variant of **Maurice.** Diminutive variant, **Morry,** sometimes occurs.

Morry: see **Morris**

Mort Independently adopted diminutive of **Mortimer** or **Morton.** Diminutive variant, **Morty,** exists.

Mortimer From surname. Regular diminutive, **Mort,** is in independent use.

Morton From surname. Diminutive variant is normally **Mort,** in independent use.

Morty: see **Mordecai** and **Mort**

Mose: see **Moses**

Moses Biblical name, from Hebrew *Mōshel,* perhaps from Egyptian *mes,* "child" or "son" (as in middle element of royal name *Rameses,* "child of Ra"). Diminutive variants include **Mo, Mose,** and **Moy.** Israeli soldier/statesman Moshe Dayan (1915–1981) had the Yiddish form of name.

Moy: see **Moses**

Muhammad Arabic name, from *muhammad,* "praiseworthy," itself from *ḥamida,* "to praise." Compare to **Ahmed.** Traditional English spelling of name was **Mahomet.**

Mungo Scottish name, perhaps from Celtic root word related to modern Welsh *mwyn,* "kind," "gentle," or "dear." No established variants.

Murgatroyd From surname. No regular variants.

Murray From Scottish surname. Few established variants, although spelling **Murry** sometimes found.

Murry: see **Murray**

Myles: see **Miles**

Myron From Greek name, meaning "myrrh." No regular variants.

Nahum Biblical name, from Hebrew *Nahūm*, "comforter." No regular variants.

Napoleon English form of Italian name *Napoleone*, perhaps originally of Germanic origin, but popularly associated with name of Naples (Italian *Napoli* from Greek *nea polis*, "new city") and Italian *leone*, "lion." No established variants.

Narcissus From Greek name *Narkissos*, itself almost certainly of pre-Greek origin, but popularly associated with Greek *narkē*, "numbness." No established variants.

Nat Independently adopted diminutive of **Nathan** or **Nathaniel**. No established variants.

Nathan Biblical name, from Hebrew *Nāthān*, "he (i.e., God) has given." Regular diminutive variant is **Nat**, in independent use. Now popularly regarded as short form of **Nathaniel**.

Nathanael: see **Nathaniel**

Nathaniel Biblical name, from Hebrew *Něthan'el*, "God has given" (compare to **Nathan**). Variant spelling, **Nathanael**, occurs. Regular diminutive is **Nat**, in independent use. **Natty** is also found, as for Natty Bumppo, central character of Fenimore Cooper's *Leatherstocking Tales* (1823–46).

Natty: see **Nathaniel**

Neal: see **Neil**

Ned Independently adopted diminutive of **Edward**, or (less often), **Edmund**. **Ted** is a related name, and **Neddy** diminutive.

Neddy: see **Ned**

Nehemiah Biblical name, from Hebrew *Něhemyāh*, "consoled by Yah" (i.e., by Jehovah). Few variants.

Neil English form of Gaelic name *Niall*, from *niadh*, "champion." Variant spellings include **Neal**, **Neill**, and **Niall**. **Nigel** is a directly related name.

Neill: see **Neil**

Nelson From surname. Few established variants.

Ner: see **Neville**

Nevil: see **Neville**

Nevile: see **Neville**

Nevill: see **Neville**

Neville From surname. Variant spellings, **Nevil**, **Nevile**, and **Nevill**, exist. Diminative **Ner** sometimes found.

Niall: see **Neil**

Nicholas English form of Greek name *Nikolaos*, comprising *nikē*, "victory," and *laos*, "people": "victorious among the people." **Nickolas** and **Nicolas** are occasional spelling variants. Regular diminutive is **Nick**, in independent use.

Nick Independently adopted diminutive of **Nicholas**. Alternate spelling, **Nik**, sometimes occurs. Regular diminutive is **Nicky**.

Nickolas: see **Nicholas**

Nicky: see **Nick**

Nicolas: see **Nicholas**

Nige: see **Nigel**

Nigel English form of medieval Latin name *Nigellus*, itself quasi-diminutive (based on *niger*, "black") of *Niel* (**Neil**). Diminutive variant, **Nige**, exists.

Nik: see **Nick**

Noah Biblical name, from Hebrew *Nōah*, traditionally said to mean "rest." No regular variants.

Noël French name, meaning "Christmas," ultimately from Latin *natalis dies* (*Domini*), "birthday (of the Lord)." Name is now usually adopted without dieresis (i.e., as Noel). (Compare to female name **Noel**.)

Norbert From Old German name, comprising *nord*, "north" and *beraht*, "bright" or "famous": "famous northman" or "famous man in the north." No regular variants, although diminutive, **Bert**, is possible.

Norm: see **Norman**

Norman From Old English name *Northmann*, "Norseman." Diminutive variant, **Norm**, is common, and **Norrie** is found in Scottish use.

Norrie: see **Norman**

Nye: see **Aneurin**

Obadiah Biblical name, from Hebrew *'Ōbadhyah*, "servant of Yah" (i.e., of Jehovah). No regular variants.

Ocky: see **Oscar**

Octavian: see **Octavius**

Octavius From Roman clan name, itself from *octavus*, "eighth." Derivative name, **Octavian**, is in occasional use.

Ogden From surname. No variants noted.

Olaf Scandinavian name, comprising *anu*, "ancestor," and *leifr*, "heir": "family descendant." Popularly (and possibly correctly) associated with **Oliver**. Variant, **Olave**, exists.

Olave: see **Olaf**

Oliver English form of French *Olivier*, popularly derived from Latin *olivarius*, "olive tree," but more likely to be of Germanic origin, akin to **Olaf**. Diminutive variants, **Noll**, **Ollie**, and **Olly**, exist, the first of these being found mostly in historical contexts.

Omar Either biblical name, from Hebrew word meaning "eloquent," or from Arabic name *'Umar*, representing *'āmir*, "flourishing" (giving English "emir"). No regular variants.

Orlando Italian form of **Roland**. No established variants.

Orson Either from surname or originally as English form of French name *Ourson*, "bear cub." Compare to female name **Ursula**. No established variants.

Orville Apparently from mock-aristocratic surname invented by Fanny Burney for Lord Orville, the central character of her novel *Evelina* (1778). No regular variants.

Osbert From Old English name *Osbeorht*, comprising ōs, "god," and *beorht*, "bright" or "famous": "famous as god." Diminutive variants **Ozzie** and **Ozzy** exist.

Osborn Either from surname, or originally from Old English name *Osbern*, itself from Scandinavian name *Asbiorn*, comprising *áss* (Old English ōs) "god," and *bjorn* (Old English *beorn*) "bear": "godlike warrior." Variant diminutives, **Ozzie** and **Ozzy**, are current.

Oscar Either from Old English name *Ansgar*, comprising ōs, "god," and *gar*, "spear": "godlike spearsman," or from Gaelic name comprising *os*, "deer," and *cara*, "friend": "gentle friend." Variant diminutives, **Ocky**, **Ozzie**, and **Ozzy**, exist.

Osmond Either from surname, or originally from Old English name *Osmund*, comprising ōs, "god," and *mund*, "protector": "protected by gods" or "godlike protector." Variant spelling, **Osmund**, occurs.

Osmund: see **Osmond**

Oswald Either from surname, or originally from Old English name *Osweald*, comprising ōs, "god," and *weald*, "rule": "godlike ruler." Diminutive variants, **Oz**, **Ozzie**, and **Ozzy**, exist.

Otis From surname, itself related to **Otto**. No established variants.

Otto German name, formed as diminutive of name containing *ot*, "prosperity" (corresponding to Old English *ēad* in names such as **Edward** and **Edwin**). No established variants.

Owen Welsh name, said to represent Latin *Eugenius* (**Eugene**). No regular variants.

Oz: see **Oswald**

Ozzie: see **Osbert, Osborne, Oscar,** and **Oswald**

Ozzy: see **Osbert, Osborn, Oscar,** and **Oswald.**

Paddy Independently adopted diminutive of **Patrick**. No regular variants.

Parker From surname. Few regular variants.

Pat Independently adopted diminutive of **Patrick**. Compare to female name **Pat**. **Patsy** is diminutive variant in independent use.

Patric: see **Patrick**

Patrick English form of Latin name *Patricius*, "patrician" (i.e., belonging to Roman nobility). Alternate spelling, **Patric**, sometimes occurs. Diminutive variants, **Paddy**, **Pat**, and **Patsy**, are in independent use.

Patsy Independently adopted diminutive of **Patrick**. Compare to female name **Patsy**. **Pat** is directly related name.

Paul Biblical name, from Latin family name *Paulus*, "small," originally a nickname. No regular variants or diminutives.

Pelham From surname. No regular variants.

Perce: see **Percy**

Percival English form of French *Perceval*, interpreted as comprising *perce*, "pierce," and *val*, "valley": "penetrator into the valley." Possibly originally Celtic name (*Peredur*) of different meaning. Probably influenced by **Percy**, although this is an unrelated name. No regular variants.

Percy From an aristocratic surname, but popularly regarded as diminutive form of **Percival**, although that is of different origin. Diminutive variant, **Perce**, occurs.

Peregrine English form of Latin name *Peregrinus*, "foreigner" or "stranger" (compare to related English "pilgrim"). Regular diminutive form, in independent use, is **Perry**.

Perry Either independently adopted diminutive of **Peregrine** or from surname. No established variants.

Pete Independently adopted diminutive of **Peter**. Few established variants.

Peter Biblical name, English form of Latin *Petrus*, itself from Greek *petros*, "rock" (compare to English "petrify" [i.e., "turn to stone"]). Regular diminutive variant is **Pete**, in independent use.

Peyton From surname. No regular variants.

Phil Independently adopted diminutive of **Philip**. Diminutive variant, **Philly**, exists, as for jazz drummer Philly Joe Jones (1923–1985).

Philemon Biblical name, from Greek name *Philēmōn*, from *philēma*, "kiss." No regular variants.

Philip Biblical name, from Greek name *Philippos*, comprising *philein*, "to love," and *hippos*, "horse": "horse-lover" or "horseman." Alternate spelling, **Phillip**, exists, while regular diminutive, **Phil**, is in independent use. Diminutive, **Pip**, also sometimes occurs in own right.

Phillip: see **Philip**

Philly: see **Phil**

Philo From Late Greek name *Philōn*, "loved," based on element *phil-* found more familiarly in **Philip**. No regular variants.

Phineas Biblical name, popularly derived from Hebrew *Pīnĕhās*, "serpent's mouth" (i.e., oracle), but more likely to be Egyptian byname originally meaning "black," (i.e., Nubian). No established variants.

Piers Medieval form of **Peter**, influenced by French *Pierre*. No regular variants.

Pip Independently adopted diminutive of **Philip**. No regular variants.

Preston From surname. No regular variants.

Prince From the royal title (compare to **Duke**, **Earl**, and **King**). No regular variants.

Quentin Independently adopted variant of **Quintin**. No regular variants.

Quincy From surname. No established variants.

Quintin English form of Latin name *Quintinus*, derivative of *Quintus*, "fifth." **Quentin** is directly related variant in independent use.

Rab: see **Robert**

Rabbie: see **Robert**

Ralph English form of Scandinavian name *Rathulfr*, with Old English equivalent *Rædulf*, comprising *ræd*, "counsel," and *wulf*, "wolf": "wise and strong." Modern spelling with *-ph* came much later through Greek classical associations (compare to **Randolph**). Usual pronunciation rhymes with "Alf," but some bearers of name prefer "Rafe." No established variants.

Randal From surname, itself a form of **Randolph**. Of the many variant spellings, **Randall** is most common in independent use. Regular diminutive, also used in own right, is **Randy**.

Randall Variant spelling of **Randal**. Regular diminutive, **Randy**, is in independent use.

Randolph From surname, itself originating as English form of Scandinavian name *Rannulfr*, with Old English equivalent *Randulf*, comprising *rand*, "edge" (i.e., of shield), and *wulf*, "wolf": "strong defender." As for **Ralph**, final *-ph* appeared much later through classical associations. Spelling variant, **Randolf**, occurs. Regular diminutive is **Randy**, in independent use.

Randy Independently adopted diminutive of **Randal** or **Randolph**. No regular variants.

Ranulf: see **Ranulph**

Ranulph English form of Scandinavian name *Reginulfr*, comprising *regin*, "advice," and *úlfr*, "wolf": "well-counseled and strong." Final *-ph* appeared later, as for **Ralph** and **Randolph**. Alternate spelling, **Ranulf**, occurs.

Raphael Biblical name, from Hebrew *Rĕphā'ēl*, "God has healed." No established variants.

Rastus: see **Erastus**

Ray Independently adopted diminutive of **Raymond**, but usually associated with "ray." No regular variants.

Raymond English form of French name *Raimont*, itself of Old German origin, comprising *ragin*, "counsel," and *mund*, "protector": "well-advised protector." Regular diminutive variant, **Ray**, is in independent use.

Rayner From surname, itself originating as Old German name *Raginhari*, comprising *ragin*, "counsel," and *hari*, "army": "well-counseled warrior." Few regular variants.

Red From nickname, often for red-haired person, or as diminutive of name beginning *R-* and ending *-d*, such as **Richard** or **Roland**. Variant spelling, **Redd**, occurs, as for actor Redd Foxx (born 1922).

Redd: see **Red**

Rees: see **Rhys**

Reg Independently adopted diminutive of **Reginald**. Diminutive variant, **Reggie**, is less common, though found for U.S. baseball player Reggie Jackson (born 1946).

Reggie: see **Reg** and **Reginald**

Reginald English form of Latin name *Reginaldus*, itself a form of **Reynold**. Regular diminutive variant is **Reg**, in independent use. **Reggie** is also found, though less frequently.

Remus From Latin name, derived by some (obscurely) from *remus*, "oar," but which, like name of *Romulus*, legendary brother and co-founder of Rome, may be linked with "Rome" itself. No variants.

René French name, from Latin name *Renatus*, "reborn." Traditional pronunciation is mostly as "Rennie," but now increasingly pronounced (especially in the U.S.) as "Renay." Compare to female name **Renée**. Now often spelled without accent (i.e., as Rene).

Reub: see **Reuben**

Reuben Biblical name, from Hebrew *Rě'ūbēn*, "behold, a son." Regular diminutive variant is **Rube**, especially in the U.S. **Reub** and **Ruby** are also found.

Rex Apparently from Latin word for "king" (compare to **King**), but always linked closely to **Reginald** (or its diminutive, **Reg**), perhaps aided by association with "regal." No established variants.

Reynold From surname, itself from Old German name comprising *ragin*, "counsel," and *wald*, "ruler": "well-counseled ruler." **Reginald** and **Ronald** are directly related names. Few, if any, variants exist.

Rhett Of uncertain origin, perhaps alteration of **Brett** or intended to suggest Greek *rhētōr*, "speaker" or "orator." No regular variants.

Rhys Welsh name, meaning "ardor" or "impetus." English version of name is **Rees**.

Richard From Old German name comprising *rīc*, "power," (modern German *Reich*, modern English "rich"), and *hart*, "strong" or "hardy": "powerful ruler." Diminutive variants, **Dick** and **Rick**, are in independent use, while **Richie** is also widely found.

Richie: see **Richard**

Rick Independently adopted diminutive of **Richard**, or (less often), of **Derek**, **Eric**, and **Frederick**. Alternate spelling, **Rik**, occurs. Diminutive, **Ricky**, is also common.

Ricky: see **Rick**

Rik: see **Rick**

Roald Norwegian name, combining *hróthr*, "fame," and *valdr*, "ruler": "famous ruler." Perhaps associated by some with **Ronald** (to which it is in fact partly related). No regular variants.

Rob: see **Robert**

Robbie: see **Robert**

Robby: see **Robert**

Robert From Old German name *Hrodebert* with Old English equivalent *Hreodbeorht*, comprising *hrōd*, "fame," and *beraht*, "bright" or "famous": (tautologically) "famed famous one." Regular diminutive, **Bob**, is independent use. Other diminutives include, **Rob**, **Robbie**, **Robby**, and Scottish **Rab** and **Rabbie**. **Rob** is also favored in Scotland. **Robin** is related name.

Robin Independently adopted historic diminutive of **Robert**, formed from *Rob* with French diminutive suffix *-in*. Compare to female name **Robin**. Few regular variants.

Rod Independently adopted diminutive of **Roderick** or **Rodney.** Diminutive variants **Roddie** and **Roddy** exist, as for British actor Roddy McDowall (born 1928), who was originally named Roderick.

Roddie: see **Rod**

Roddy: see **Rod**

Roderic: see **Roderick**

Roderick English form of Old German name *Hrodrich*, comprising *hrōd*, "fame," and *rīc*, "power": "famously powerful." Variant spelling is **Roderic**, and regular diminutive is **Rod**, in independent use.

Rodger: see **Roger**

Rodney From surname. Regular diminutive variant, **Rod**, is in independent use.

Rog: see **Roger**

Roger English form (through French) of Old German name *Hrodgar*, with Old English equivalent *Hrōthgār*, comprising *hrōd*, "fame," and *gēr*, "spear": "famous warrior." Variant spelling, **Rodger**, is sometimes found, while usual diminutive is **Rog** (pronounced "Rodge").

Roland English form (through French) of Old German name *Hrōdland*, comprising *hrōd*, "fame," and *lant*, "land" or "territory": "famous landowner." Variant spelling, **Rowland**, is in independent use.

Rolf English contraction of original Old German name that gave **Rudolph**. Variant spelling, **Rolph**, sometimes occurs.

Rolph: see **Rolf**

Roman From Late Latin name *Romanus*, "Roman" or "man from Rome." No regular variants.

Romeo Italian name, meaning "one who has made pilgrimage to Rome." No established variants.

Ron Independently adopted diminutive of **Ronald**. Diminutive variant, **Ronnie**, is in independent use.

Ronald English form of Old Norse name *Rögnvaldr*, equivalent in meaning to Old German name **Reynold**, (which itself gave **Reginald**). Regular diminutive variants, both in independent use, are **Ron** and **Ronnie**.

Ronnie Independently adopted diminutive of **Ron** or **Ronald**. No regular variants.

Rory English form of Gaelic name *Ruaidhrí* comprising Old Celtic words corresponding to modern Irish *rua*, "red," and *rí*, "king": "great king" or "famous ruler." No regular variants.

Ross From Scottish surname. No regular variants.

Rowan From Irish surname. No established variants.

Rowland Either from surname, or independently adopted variant of **Roland** (which gave that surname). Few established variants.

Roy English form of Gaelic name *Ruadh*, "red," i.e., "red-haired": "outstanding" or "famous." Now commonly associated with Old French *roy* (modern French *roi*), "king" (compare to **King**, **Leroy**, and **Rufus**). No regular variants.

Rube: see **Reuben**

Ruby: see **Reuben**

Rudolf: see **Rudolph**

Rudolph From Old German name *Hrōdulf*, comprising *hrōd*, "fame," and *wulf*, "wolf": "famous warrior" (exactly as for **Rolf**). The *-ph* appears much later through classical associations. Alternate spelling, **Rudolf**, exists.

Rufus Biblical name, from Latin name meaning "red" or "red-haired": "prominent" (compare to **Roy**). No regular variants.

Rupert English form of German name *Ruprecht*, itself from Old German *Hrodebert*, which gave **Robert**. Few established variants or diminutives.

Russ Independently adopted diminutive of **Russell**. No regular variants.

Russell From surname. Regular diminutive variant is **Russ**, used in own right.

Rutland From surname. No established variants.

Ryan From Irish surname. No established variants.

Sacha: see **Sasha**

Sam Independently adopted diminutive of **Samuel**, or (less often), **Samson**. Diminutive variant is **Sammy,** in independent use.

Sammy Independently adopted diminutive of **Sam** or **Samuel**. No regular variants.

Sampson Either from surname or independently adopted variant of **Samson**. Diminutive variant is normally **Sam,** in independent use.

Samson Biblical name, from Hebrew *Shimshōn,* diminutive of *shemesh,* "sun." **Sampson** is spelling variant in independent use. Regular diminutive is **Sam**.

Samuel Biblical name, from Hebrew *Shēmū'ēl,* "name of God" (literally, "his name is El"). (Interpretation "asked for" in 1 Samuel 1:20 is more suited to **Saul**.) Regular diminutive variant, **Sam,** is in independent use.

Sandy Independently adopted diminutive of **Alexander,** possibly influenced by "sandy," as this is typical hair color of Scottish people. Compare to female name **Sandy**. No regular variants.

Sasha English adoption of Russian diminutive of **Alexander**. Compare to female name **Sasha**. French variant, **Sacha,** made known by French popular singer Sacha Distel (born 1933). Diminutive, **Sy,** exists, as for screenwriter Sy Bartlett (1900–1978), whose original first name was Sacha.

Saul Biblical name, from Hebrew *Shā'ūl*, "asked for" or "desired" (i.e., of God). (See also **Samuel**.) No established variants.

Scott From Scottish surname. Usual diminutive variants are **Scottie** and **Scotty**.

Scottie: see **Scott**

Scotty: see **Scott**

Seamas: see **Seamus**

Seamus English form of Irish name *Séamas* (**James**), pronounced "*Shay*mus." Alternate spellings, **Seamas** and **Seumas**, exist.

Sean English form of Irish name *Seán* (**John**), pronounced "Shawn." **Shane** is directly related name, and common spelling variants are **Shaun** (mostly in the U.K.) and **Shawn** (mostly in the U.S.).

Seb: see **Sebastian**

Sebastian English form of Greek name *Sebastianos*, "man from Sebasta" (a city in Asia Minor), but also linked with Greek *sebastos*, "reverenced" or "august" (compare to **Augustus**). Association with "bastion" also sometimes made. Regular diminutive variant is **Seb**, but **Baz** and **Bazza** are also found.

Selwin: see **Selwyn**

Selwyn From surname. Variant spelling, **Selwin**, occasionally occurs.

Septimus From Late Latin name meaning "seventh." No established variants.

Seth Biblical name, from Hebrew *Shēth*, "appointed" or "set." No established variants.

Seumas: see **Seamus**

Seymour From surname. No established variants.

Shane Either from Irish surname or English form of Irish name, **Sean**, which gave surname. Spelling variants are as for **Sean**.

Shaun: see **Sean**

Shawn: see **Sean**

Sheldon From surname. No established variants.

Shem Biblical name, from Hebrew word meaning "name" (compare to **Samuel**). No variants noted.

Sheridan From Irish surname. No regular variants.

Sholto English form of Scottish Gaelic name *Sìoltach*, "sower" (i.e., metaphorically "fruitful" or "producing many offspring"). No regular variants.

Sid Independently adopted diminutive of **Sidney**. No regular variants.

Sidney From surname. Variant spelling, **Sydney**, is in independent use, as is regular diminutive, **Sid**.

Siggy: see **Sigmund**

Sigmund From Old German name comprising *sigu*, "victory," and *munt*, "defender": "victorious defender" or "protector of victory." Diminutive variant, **Siggy**, exists.

Silas Biblical name, from Latin *Silvanus*, itself from *silva*, "wood," implying a person who lived in or by the woods. No established variants.

Silvester Latin name, from *silvestris*, "of the woods" or "rural," derivative of *silva*, "wood." Variant spelling, **Sylvester**, is in independent use.

Sim: see **Simon**

Simeon Biblical name, from Hebrew *Shim'ōn*, "he who hears." **Simon** is directly related name.

Simmy: see **Simon**

Simon Biblical name, English form of **Simeon**, with same Hebrew origin, but popularly also associated with Greek *simos*, "snub-nosed." Diminutive variants, **Sim** and **Simmy**, exist.

Sinclair From Scottish surname. No regular variants.

Sol: see **Solomon**

Solly: see **Solomon**

Solomon Biblical name, from Hebrew *Shĕlōmōh*, itself from *shālōm*, "peace": "man of peace." Standard diminutive variants are **Sol** and **Solly**, later as for South African-born British scientist Solly Zuckerman (born 1904).

Sonnie: see **Sonny**

Sonny Either independently adopted diminutive from names such as **Saul** or **Solomon**, or general nickname for young person. Often associated with **Sunny**. Variant spelling, **Sonnie**, exists.

Spencer From surname. No regular variants.

Spike From nickname, either for someone with "spiky" hair or for any person generally. No regular variants.

Stacey: see **Stacy**

Stacy From surname, itself derivative of **Eustace**. Compare to female name **Stacy**. Variant spelling, **Stacey**, occurs.

Stafford From surname. No regular variants.

Stan Independently adopted diminutive of **Stanley**. Few established variants.

Stanley From surname. Regular diminutive variant is **Stan**, in independent use.

Stephen Biblical name, English form of Greek name *Stephanos*, "garland" or "crown." Variant spelling, **Steven**, is in independent use, as is regular diminutive, **Steve**.

Sterling From surname, with suggestion of "sterling" meaning "excellent value." Variant spelling, **Stirling**, is in independent use.

Steve Independently adopted diminutive of **Stephen** or **Steven**. Diminutive variant, **Stevie**, is frequent, as for singer/ songwriter Stevie Wonder (born 1950), whose original first name was Steveland.

Stevie: see **Steve**

Stew: see **Stuart**

Stewart Either from Scottish surname, or as independently adopted variant of **Stuart**. Diminutive variants, **Stew** and **Stu**, are in common use.

Stu: see **Stewart**

Stuart From Scottish surname, itself French form of surname **Stewart**. Diminutive variants, **Stew** and **Stu**, are commonly found.

Sunny From the ordinary word, implying cheerful personality, but also often influenced by **Sonny**. No regular variants.

Swithin From Old English name *Suitha*, based on *swīth*, "strong" or "mighty." No recorded variants.

Sy: see **Sasha**

Syd: see **Sydney**

Sydney Independently adopted variant of **Sidney**. Diminutive variant, **Syd**, exists, but is not as common as **Sid**, in independent use.

Syl: see **Sylvester**

Sylvester Independently adopted diminutive of **Silvester**. Diminutive variants, **Syl** and **Vester**, both exist.

Tad: see **Thaddeus**

Taff: see **Taffy**

Taffy English form of Welsh *Dafydd* (**David**), independently adopted as diminutive. Diminutive variant, **Taff**, also exists.

Talbot From surname. No regular variants.

Ted Independently adopted diminutive of **Edward**, or (less often), **Theodore**. Regular diminutive variant, **Teddy**, is in independent use.

Teddie: see **Teddy**

Teddy Independently adopted diminutive of **Edward**, **Theodore**, or **Ted**. Spelling variant, **Teddie**, occasionally occurs.

Tel: see **Terry**

Terence English form of Latin name *Terentius*, of uncertain origin (perhaps associated with *terere*, "to rub," "to wear out," or "to use up"). Variant spellings, **Terrance** and **Terrence**, occur. Regular diminutive, **Terry**, is in independent use.

Terrance: see **Terence**

Terrence: see **Terence**

Terry Either from surname, or as independently adopted diminutive of **Terence**. Compare to female name **Terry**. Regular diminutive variant is **Tel**.

Tex From nickname for person from Texas, perhaps prompted by names such as **Ted, Dexter, Lex,** and **Rex.** Few regular variants.

Thad: see **Thaddeus**

Thaddeus Biblical name, perhaps form of Greek name *Theodōros* (**Theodore**). Variant spelling, **Thadeus,** occurs, with diminutives **Tad** and **Thad** existing, the latter as for composer Thad Jones (1923–1986).

Thadeus: see **Thaddeus**

Theo Independently adopted diminutive of **Theodore,** or (less often), **Theobald.** No regular variants.

Theobald English form of ultimately Old German name, comprising *theud,* "people" or "race," and *bald,* "bold" or "brave": "brave man." The first part of the name is altered by association with Greek *theos,* "god," found in other names such as **Theodore** and **Theophilus.** Regular diminutive form, where used, is **Theo,** adopted in own right.

Theodore English form of Greek name *Theodōros,* comprising *theos,* "god," and *dōron,* "gift": (in Christian terms) "God's gift" (i.e., of a child). Regular diminutive variants are **Ted, Teddy,** and **Theo,** all in independent use.

Theophilus Biblical name, Latin form of Greek name *Theophilos,* comprising *theos,* "god," and *philos,* "friend": (for Christians) "one who loves God" or "loved by God." Regular diminutive variant, where used, is **Theo,** adopted independently.

Thomas Biblical name, Greek form of Aramaic byname *Tĕ'ōma,* "twin." Regular diminutive variants are **Tom** and **Tommy,** in independent use.

Thurston From surname. No regular variants.

Tim Independently adopted diminutive of **Timothy**. Diminutive variant, **Timmy**, is also current, but associated more with young boys than grown men.

Timmy: see **Tim**

Timothy Biblical name, English form of Greek name *Timotheos*, comprising *tīmē*, "honor," and *theos*, "god": "honored by God" or "honoring God." Regular diminutive variant is **Tim**, in independent use.

Tiny From nickname, either for small (or very tall) person, or from some incident. No established variants, though facetious form "Tina" sometimes occurs, from female name, as for jazzman Tina Brooks (1932–1974), whose original first names were Harold Floyd.

Titus Biblical name, of uncertain origin, but perhaps from Latin *titulus*, "title of honor." No established variants.

Tobias Biblical name, from Hebrew *Tōbhīyāh*, "Yah (i.e., Jehovah) is good." Diminutive variant of name, **Toby**, is in independent use.

Toby Independently adopted diminutive (or variant) of **Tobias**. No established variants.

Tod: see **Todd**

Todd From surname. Variant spelling **Tod** also found, especially in the U.S.

Tom Independently adopted diminutive of **Thomas**. Diminutive, **Tommy**, is in independent use.

Tommie: see **Tommy**

Tommy Independently adopted diminutive of **Thomas** or **Tom**. Variant spelling, **Tommie**, sometimes occurs.

Tone: see **Tony**

Tony Independently adopted diminutive of **Anthony** or **Antony**. Variant diminutive, **Tone**, occasionally occurs.

Tracy From surname. Compare to female name **Tracy**. No regular variants.

Trev: see **Trevor**

Trevor From Welsh surname. Usual diminutive variant is **Trev**.

Tris: see **Tristram**

Tristan: see **Tristram**

Tristram Of uncertain Celtic derivation, perhaps related to *drest* or *drust* (modern Welsh *drwst*), "noise" or "din," but long popularly associated with Latin *tristis*, mainly through tragic legend of Tristram and Isolde. Most common variant is **Tristan**, also found in legend. Diminutive, **Tris**, occasionally occurs, as for baseball player Tris Speaker (1885–1958).

Troy Probably from surname, but popularly associated with ancient city of Troy. No regular variants.

Truman From surname. No regular variants.

Tudor From surname, English form of Welsh name *Tudur*, itself from Old Celtic name *Teutorix*, comprising elements meaning respectively "people," "tribe," and "ruler" or "king": "people's ruler." Usually associated with **Theodore**, but that is a different name, of Greek origin.

Ulysses Latin form, much altered, of Greek name *Odysseus*, perhaps related to *odyssesthai*, "to hate." No established variants.

Urban Biblical name, English form of Latin name *Urbanus*, "from the city" or "urban." No regular variants.

Uriah Biblical name, from Hebrew *Ūrīyāh*, "Yah (i.e., Jehovah) is light" (compare to **Uriel**). No established variants.

Uriel Biblical name, from Hebrew *Ūrī'ēl*, "God is light" (compare to **Uriah**). No established variants.

Val Independently adopted diminutive of **Valentine**. Compare to female name **Val**. No regular variants.

Valentine English form of Latin name *Valentinus*, itself from *valens*, genitive *valentis*, "healthy" or "strong." Diminutive variant, **Val**, is in occasional independent use.

Van Independently adopted diminutive of **Evan**, **Ivan**, and **Vance**, or from surname Van or even element *van* "of," in Dutch surname. No regular variants.

Vance From surname. Few established variants though **Van** can evolve.

Vaughan From Welsh surname. Variant spelling, **Vaughn**, also occurs, as for bandleader Vaughn Monroe (1911–1973).

Vaughn: see **Vaughan**

Vergil Independently adopted variant of **Virgil**. No regular variants.

Vern: see **Vernon**

Vernon From surname. Diminutive variant, **Vern**, sometimes occurs.

Vester: see **Sylvester**

Vic Independently adopted diminutive of **Victor**. Variant spelling, **Vick**, also found, together with diminutive, **Vicky**.

Vick: see **Vic** and **Victor**

Vicky: see **Vic** and Victor

Victor From late Latin name meaning "victor" or "conqueror" (compare to **Vincent**). Diminutive variant, **Vic**, is in independent use. **Vicky** also exists.

Vince: see **Vincent**

Vincent Either from surname or as English form (through French) of Latin name *Vincens*, genitive *Vincentis*, "conquering" or "victorious" (compare to **Victor**). Diminutive variant, **Vince**, occurs.

Virgil From Roman clan name *Vergilius*, later spelled *Virgilius* by association with Latin *virgo*, "maiden" or *virga*, "stick." No established variants.

Viv: see **Vivian**

Vivian English form of Latin name *Vivianus*, of uncertain origin (but perhaps from *vivus*, "alive"). Variant spelling, **Vyvyan**, is in independent use, and usual diminutive is **Viv**.

Vyv: see **Vyvyan**

Vyvyan From surname, itself a form of **Vivian**. Few regular variants, although diminutive, **Vyv**, would logically evolve.

Waldo From short form of Old German name containing *wald*, "rule," such as **Walter**. No regular variants.

Wallace From (mainly) Scottish surname. Regular diminutive variant is **Wally**, in independent use.

Wally Independently adopted diminutive of **Wallace** or **Walter**. Few regular variants.

Walt Independently adopted diminutive of **Walter**. No regular variants.

Walter From Old German name comprising *wald*, "rule," and *heri*, "army": "army ruler." Diminutives in independent use are **Wally** and **Walt** (also formerly **Wat**).

Ward From surname. No established variants.

Warren From surname. No regular variants.

Washington From surname. No established variants.

Wat Independently adopted diminutive of **Walter**. Variant spelling, **Watt**, sometimes occurs.

Watt: see **Wat**

Wayne From surname. No regular variants.

Webster From surname. No regular variants.

Wendell From surname. No established variants.

Wes: see **Wesley**

Wesley From surname. Diminutive variant, **Wes**, exists.

Whitney From surname. Compare to female name **Whitney**. Few regular variants.

Wilbur From surname. Few established variants.

Wilf: see **Wilfred** and **Wilfrid**

Wilfred Independently adopted variant of **Wilfrid**. Diminutive variant, **Wilf**, is in regular use.

Wilfrid From Old English name *Wilfridh*, comprising *will*, "will" or "desire," and *frithu*, "peace": "desirer of peace" or "peacelover." Variant spelling, **Wilfred**, is in independent use. Regular diminutive is **Wilf**.

Wilkie From surname, but commonly felt to be diminutive of names such as **Wilfred** or **William**. Few regular variants.

Will Independently adopted diminutive of **William**. Diminutive variants, **Willie** and **Willy**, exist.

William From Old German name comprising *willo*, "will" or "desire," and *helm*, "helmet" or "protection": "one who desires to protect" or "defender." Diminutive variants, **Bill**, **Will**, and **Willie**, are in independent use.

Willie Independently adopted diminutive of **William**, or (less often), other name beginning *Will-*. Alternate spelling, **Willy**, also exists.

Willoughby From surname. Few established variants.

Willy: see **Will** and **Willie**

Windsor From surname. No established variants.

Winnie: see **Winston**

Winston From surname. Diminutive variant, **Winnie**, exists.

Wolf Either short form of German name such as *Wolfgang*, or from surname, or even directly from *Wolf*, (i.e., the animal). No established variants.

Woodrow From surname. **Woody** is common diminutive.

Woody Independently adopted diminutive of **Woodrow**, suggesting a connection with woods or forests (compare to **Silas** and **Silvester**). No regular variants.

Wyatt From surname. No recorded variants.

Wyndham From surname. No regular variants.

Xavier From name of Spanish soldier, founder of Jesuits, St. Francis Xavier (1506–1552). Few established variants.

York From surname. No recorded variants.

Zacchaeus Biblical name, from Hebrew *Zakkai*, "innocent" or "justified." No regular variants, although diminutive, **Zack**, is possible, as for **Zachary.**

Zachariah Alteration of biblical name Zachariah, from Hebrew *Zĕkharyah*, "Yah (i.e., Jehovah) has remembered." **Zachary** is directly derived name, and **Zacharias** is variant. Usual diminutive is **Zack.**

Zacharias: see **Zachariah**

Zachary English form of Greek name *Zacharias*, representing biblical name **Zachariah**. Regular diminutive variants are **Zack** and **Zak**. Latter was given to first son (born 1965) of former Beatle, Ringo Starr (born 1940).

Zack: see **Zacchaeus, Zachariah,** and **Zachary**

Zak: see **Isaac** and **Zachery**

Zeb: see **Zebedee**

Zebedee Biblical name, English alternate form of biblical name Zebadiah, itself from Hebrew *Zĕbhadhyāhu*, "Yah (i.e., Jehovah) has given." Diminutive variant, **Zeb**, exists.

Zed: see **Zedekiah**

Zedekiah Biblical name, from Hebrew *Tsidhqīyāhu*, "Yah (i.e., Jehovah) is just." Diminutive variant, **Zed**, has been recorded.

Zeke: see **Ezekiel**

Zeph: see **Zephaniah**

Zephaniah Biblical name, from Hebrew *Tsephanyāh*, "Yah (i.e., Jehovah) has hidden." Diminutive variant, more common than full form, is **Zeph**.

Girls

Abbey: see **Abigail**

Abbie: see **Abigail**

Abby: see **Abigail**

Abigail Biblical name, from Hebrew *Abīgayil*, "(my) father rejoices." Variants include **Abbey**, **Abbie**, and **Abby**. There also exists independently adopted diminutive, **Gail**.

Ad: see **Ada**

Ada From first element, *adal*, "noble," of Old German name such as *Adalheit* (**Adelaide**). Perhaps also influenced by **Adah**. Variants include **Ad**, **Addie**, and **Adie**.

Adah Biblical name, from Hebrew *Ādāh*, "ornamented" or "decorated." Later associated with **Ada**. No regular variants.

Addi: see **Adeline**

Addie: see **Ada**

Addy: see **Adeline**

Adela Like **Ada**, from Old German *adal*, "noble," as in *Adalheit* (**Adelaide**). Variants include independently adopted **Adele**, and alternate spelling, **Adella**.

Adella: see **Adela**

Adelaide English form (through French) of Old German name *Adalheit*, comprising *adal*, "noble," and *heit*, "state" or "condition": "woman of noble estate." Many variants gained independent use, especially **Ada**, **Adela**, **Adele**, and **Adeline**. **Alice** and **Heidi** are directly related names.

Adele Independently adopted French diminutive of **Adelaide** or similar name beginning with element *adal*, "noble." Main variant is **Adèle** (with accent). Variant spelling, **Adelle**, is also found.

Adèle: see **Adele**

Adelina: see **Adeline**

Adeline Like **Adelaide**, a French form, influenced by **Adele**, of Old German *Adalheit*, "woman of noble estate." Variants include **Addi**, **Addy**, and **Aline**. An Italian form, **Adelina**, also exists.

Adella: see **Adela**

Adelle: see **Adele**

Adie: see **Ada**

Adriana: see **Adrienne**

Adriane: see **Adrienne**

Adrianne: see **Adrienne**

Adrienne French female equivalent of **Adrian**. Variants include **Adriana**, **Adriane**, and **Adrianne**, with the latter perhaps being influenced by **Ann**.

Agatha From Greek *agathē*, feminine of *agathos*, "good." Diminutive variant, **Aggie**, exists, as for **Agnes**.

Aggie: see **Agatha** and **Agnes**

Agnes From Greek *hagnos*, "pure" or "chaste," also influenced by Latin *agnus*, "lamb," with association of meaning as well as words. Variants include **Aggie**, **Nessie**, and **Nesta**, with the latter in independent use.

Aileen: see **Eileen**

Ailsa Scottish name, probably from rocky islet Ailsa Craig in Firth of Clyde, but influenced by (and commonly regarded as variant of) **Elsa**. No regular variants.

Aimée From French *aimée*, "beloved," equivalent to English **Amy**. Variant spelling is **Aimi**.

Aimi: see **Aimée**

Alberta Feminine form of male name **Albert**. There exist few established variants, although **Bertie** would be a logical diminutive.

Aleta: see **Alethea**

Aletha: see **Alethea**

Alethea From Greek *alētheia*, "truth," but sometimes associated with **Althea**, although that has a different origin. Variants, **Aleta** and **Aletha**, occur, with diminutive, **Letty**, which also evolves from **Letitia**.

Alex: see **Alexandra**

Alexa: see **Alexandra**

Alexandra Feminine form of **Alexander**. Many variants exist, mainly as shortenings or diminutives, such as **Alex**, **Alexa**, **Alexia**, and **Alexis**, with the latter in independent use. **Lexy** is also found. Diminutives, **Sandra** and **Sasha**, now are independently used. All variants are currently most commonly used in Scotland.

Alexia: see **Alexandra**

Alexis Female adoption of identical male name, itself ultimately from Greek name *Alexios*, a short form of **Alexander** or similar name based on *alexein*, "to defend." Now regarded as short form of **Alexandra**. Variants are mostly as for **Alexandra** itself.

Ali: see **Alice** and **Alison**

Alice Like **Adelaide**, a French form, in this case much "smoothed," of Old German name *Adalheit*, "woman of noble estate." Variants include **Alicia**, **Alisa**, **Alissa**, and **Alyssa**. **Alison** is an independent name. Diminutive, **Ali**, is found, as for actress Ali McGraw (born 1938).

Alicia: see **Alice**

Aline: see **Adeline**

Alisa: see **Alice**

Alison French diminutive form of **Alice**. Variants include **Allison** and **Alyson**, with usual diminutive, **Ali**.

Alissa: see **Alice**

Allegra From feminine of Italian word *allegro*, "gay" or "happy." No regular variants.

Allison: see **Alison**

Alma From Latin *alma*, "kind" or "nurturing," but subsequently associated with Italian *alma*, "soul." No regular variants.

Althea From Greek name *Althaia*, itself from Greek *althein*, "to heal." Commmonly associated with **Alethea**, but that name has a different origin. Few regular variants.

Alva Adoption of male name **Alva**, regarded by some as feminine equivalent of **Alvin**. Rare alternate spelling, **Alvah**, exists.

Alvah: see **Alva**

Alyson: see **Alison**

Alyssa: see **Alice**

Amabel English derivative of Latin *amabilis*, "lovable" (compare to **Amanda**). Best-known diminutive, **Mabel**, is long established as name in own right. Name also influenced **Annabel**.

Amanda Ultimately from feminine form of Latin saint's name *Amandus*, "fit to be loved." Most popular variant is **Mandy**, adopted for independent use.

Amaryllis Greek name, perhaps from *amaryssein*, "to sparkle," as of flowing water. No regular variants.

Amber From the jewel. No established variants.

Amelia Probably blended name, from Roman clan name *Aemilius*, which gave **Emily**, and first element, *amal*, "industrious," of Old German name such as *Amalberga*. Variants include independently adopted **Emilia**, diminutives, **Millie** and **Milly**, latter also evolving from **Millicent**.

Amey: see **Amy**

Amie: see **Amy**

Amy From Old French *amee* (modern *aimée*), "beloved" (compare to **Aimée** and **Amanda**). Variant spellings are **Amey** and **Amie**, with the latter often being associated with French *amie*, "(female) friend."

Anastasia Feminine form of Greek name *Anastasius*, itself from *anastasis*, "resurrection." Long name has generated briefer variants, most popular being diminutive, **Stacy**, now used independently.

Andie: see **Andrea**

Andrea Regarded as regular feminine form of **Andrew**, perhaps under Italian influence. Variants include **Andie** and **Andy**, as for **Andrew**, with French variant, **Andrée**, found almost as frequently.

Andrée: see **Andrea**

Andy: see **Andrea**

Ange: see **Angel** and **Angela**

Angel Either feminine adoption of male name **Angel**, or directly from standard word. Few regular variants, although diminutives, **Ange** and **Angie**, are possible.

Angela Feminine form of male name **Angel**. One of the best-known variants, **Angelica**, is now an independent name. Others are **Angelina** and **Angeline**, with diminutives, **Angie**, **Angy**, and **Ange**, in use.

Angelica Ultimately from feminine form of Latin *angelicus*, "angelic," but now regarded as a diminutive of **Angela**. Variant spellings are French **Angelique** (**Angélique**), and more recently **Anjelica**, as for actress Anjelica Huston (born 1952). **Angelina** is a directly related variant.

Angelina Latin-style form of **Angelica**. Variant form is **Angeline**, with usual diminutive, **Angie**.

Angeline English adoption of French equivalent of **Angelina**. Usual diminutive is **Angie**.

Angelique: see **Angelica**

Angélique: see **Angelica**

Angharad Welsh name, comprising *an*, intensifying particle, and *câr*, "love": "much loved." Pronunciation is approximately "An*har*ad." No regular variants.

Angie: see **Angel, Angela, Angelina**, and **Angeline**

Angy: see **Angela**

Anita Spanish diminutive of *Ana* (**Ann**). Variant, **Nita**, is fairly common diminutive.

Anjelica: see **Angelica**

Ann English form of biblical name **Hannah**, so like it, means "grace" or "favor." French variant of name, **Anne**, is now equally popular. Diminutives, **Annie, Nan, Nana**, and **Nancy**, are in independent use, as are many continental European diminutives, such as Spanish **Anita**, Swedish **Anneka**, and French **Annette. Anne-Marie** (Annemaria) is common French and German combination. The name also occurs as second half of dual names such as **Jo Ann** and **Mary Ann** (also found with hyphen), and is often felt to be distinct element in names such as independent **Joanne** and **Marianne.**

Anna From Greek or Latin form of **Hannah**, as for **Ann**, now common in many European languages. Main variants are as for **Ann** itself.

Annabel Probably alteration of **Amabel**, "bel" being associated with French *belle*, "beautiful." Now sometimes felt to be compound name with **Ann** or **Anna** as first part. Main variants are **Annabella** and **Annabelle**, as if to emphasize "beautiful" association.

Annabella: see **Annabel**

Annabelle: see **Annabel**

Anne-Marie: see **Ann**

Anne: see **Ann**

Anneka Swedish diminutive of **Ann**. Variant spelling, **Annika**, is sometimes found, with usual diminutive, **Annie**.

Annett: see **Annette**

Annetta: see **Annette**

Annette French diminutive of **Ann**. Variant forms are **Annetta** and **Annett**.

Annie Independently adopted diminutive of **Ann**. Few further variants.

Annika: see **Anneka**

Anona Of uncertain origin. Perhaps blend of names such as **Ann** and **Fiona**. No regular variants.

Anthea From Greek name *Antheia*, itself feminine of Greek *antheios*, "flowery." Few regular variants.

Antonia Feminine form of male **Anthony** (Antony). Best-known variant is French **Antoinette**, familiar from Marie-Antoinette (1755–1793), queen of France by marriage to Louis XVI. Diminutive in independent use is **Toni**.

Antoinette: see **Antonia**

April From the month, considered as one of the most

attractive of the year, implying new birth and blossoming. Best-known variant is independently adopted **Avril**. **Averil** is also sometimes regarded as variant, but is really a distinct name.

Arabel: see **Arabella**

Arabell: see **Arabella**

Arabella Probably alteration of **Annabella**, early form (now a variant) of **Annabel**, although attempts have been made to see derivation in Latin *orabilis*, "entreatable," as Orabilis was early doublet for some women named **Arabella**. Variants are mainly spelling permutations such as **Arabel** and **Arabell**, but diminutives, **Bella** and **Belle**, also exist, and are now in independent use.

Araminta Origin uncertain, perhaps blend of **Arabella** and rare name Aminta. No regular variants, but diminutive, **Minta**, exists.

Aretha Form of Greek name *Arete*, representing *aretē*, "excellence" (compare to **Arethusa**, of which it could also be a diminutive). No regular variants.

Arethusa Greek name, perhaps based on *aretē*, "excellence." No established variants.

Ariadne Greek name, perhaps deriving from intensive prefix *ari-*, and *agnos*, "pure" or "chaste": "very pure." No regular variants.

Arleen: see **Arlene**

Arlena: see **Arlene**

Arlene Probably independent development from **Charlene** or **Marlene**. Variants include **Arlena**, **Arline**, and **Arleen**.

Arlette French name of uncertain origin. Perhaps a derivative of **Charlotte**. No regular variants.

Arline: see **Arlene**

Aspasia Greek name, meaning "welcomed one." Spelling variant is **Aspatia**.

Aspatia: see **Aspasia**

Asta: see **Astrid**

Astrid From Old Norse name *Astrithr*, comprising *ans*, "god," and *frithr*, "fair": "divinely beautiful." Best-known variant is diminutive, **Asta**.

Aubrey Female adoption of male name **Aubrey**. No regular variants.

Aud: see **Audrey**

Audi: see **Audrey**

Audie: see **Audrey**

Audrey Much "smoothed" variant of Old English *Æthelthryth*, comprising *æthele*, "noble," and *thrȳth*, "strength": "noble strength." Variants and diminutives include **Aud, Audi, Audie, Audrie,** and **Audry**.

Audrie: see **Audrey**

Audry: see **Audrey**

Augusta Feminine form of **Augustus** (or in some cases, **Augustin**). Roman emperors assumed title *Augustus* ("venerable" or "august") on their accession, and *Augusta* was title of honor then given to their wives, daughters, and other female relatives. Variants include French form **Auguste**, diminutives, **Augustina** and **Augustine**, and short forms, **Gus** and **Gussie**.

Auguste: see **Augusta**

Augustina: see **Augusta**

Augustine: see **Augusta**

Aurelia Feminine of Latin clan name *Aurelius*, itself ultimately from *aurum*, "gold." No regular variants.

Aurie: see **Auriol**

Auriel: see **Auriol**

Auriol From feminine of Latin *aureolus*, diminutive of *aureus*, "golden." Linked also with Roman clan name *Aurelius*, as for **Aurelia**. Variant spellings, **Auriel** and **Auriole**, exist, with diminutives, **Aurie** and **Aury**.

Auriole: see **Auriol**

Aurora From name of Roman goddess of dawn, meaning "dawn" itself. Best-known variant is French **Aurore**.

Aurore: see **Aurora**

Aury: see **Auriol**

Ava Probably development from **Eva**, independent variant of **Eve**, but commonly associated with Latin *avis*, "bird." No regular variants.

Avaril: see **Averil**

Aveline Probably French diminutive of *Avila*, itself name of Old German origin related to **Avis**. (See also **Eileen**.) No established variants.

Averil Probably independently adopted variant of **Avril**, but could also have developed from Old English name *Eoforhild*, comprising *eofor,* "boar," and *hild,* "battle": "boarlike in battle." Variants are mainly alternate spellings, such as **Avaril** and **Averill**.

Averill: see **Averil**

Avice Independently adopted variant of **Avis**, pronounced with short "a," as in **Alice**. No regular variants.

Avis Ultimate origin uncertain, but perhaps relating to German name *Hedwig*, both parts of which mean "struggle." Now associated with Latin *avis,* "bird." Usually pronounced with long "a," as in **Mavis**. Best-known variant is independently adopted **Avice**.

Avril Either from French *avril,* (**April**), or like **Averil**, developing from Old English name *Eoforhild*. Variants are as for **Averil** itself.

Azalea From the flower. No regular variants.

Bab: see **Barbara**

Babette: see **Barbara**

Babs: see **Barbara**

Bar: see **Barbara**

Barbar: see **Barbara**

Barbara Feminine of Greek *barbaros*, "strange" or "foreign," a word representing the stammering used by a person who did not speak Greek. Variants include **Bab, Babs,** French **Babette, Bar, Barbie** (popular from the doll), and **Barbar.**

Barbie: see **Barbara**

Bathsheba Biblical name, from Hebrew *Bathsheba'* meaning either "daughter of oath" or "seventh daughter." Most familiar variant is **Sheba,** adopted in its own right.

Bea: see **Beatrice**

Beatrice From Latin *beatrix*, genitive *beatricis*, "she who makes happy," itself from *beatus*, "blessed" or "lucky." Most common variant is **Beatrix,** in independent use. Common diminutive is **Bea. Trixie** is diminutive in independent use.

Beatrix Directly from Latin *beatrix*, "she who makes happy," which also gave **Beatrice.** Diminutive variant, **Trixie,** is in independent use.

Becky Independently adopted diminutive of **Rebecca**. No established variants.

Bel: see **Belinda**

Belinda Perhaps ultimately derived from Old German word *lint*, "snake," alluding to cunning, but otherwise of obscure origin. Could be blend of Italian *bella* or French *belle*, "beautiful," and name such as **Lucinda**, but now more obviously associated with **Bella** and **Linda**. Main variant is diminutive, **Bel**.

Bella Both a derivative of names such as **Arabella** and **Isabel**, and an adoption of the word for "beautiful" in a Romance language (such as Spanish *bella* or French *belle*). Main variant is French equivalent, **Belle**, in select independent use.

Belle Independently adopted variant of **Bella**, exactly reflecting French *belle*, "beautiful." No regular variants. Addition of diminutive suffix would suggest "belly."

Berenice: see **Bernice**

Bernadette Feminine form of **Bernard**. Diminutive sometimes found is **Detta**.

Bernice Biblical name, ultimately from Greek name *Pherenīkē*, "bringing victory." Formerly believed to be variant of **Veronica**, but that is a different name. Best-known variant is **Berenice**, former usual form of name. Diminutives include **Bernie**, **Berry**, **Binnie**, and **Bunny**.

Bernie: see **Bernice**

Berry: see **Bernice** and **Beryl**

Bert: see **Bertha**

Berta: see **Bertha** and **Roberta**

Bertha From Old German name *Berahta*, itself from *beraht*, "bright" or "famous." French variant, **Berthe**, is occasionally found. Others are **Berta, Bertie, Bertina**, or the simple diminutive, **Bert**.

Berthe: see **Bertha**

Bertie: see **Alberta** and **Bertha**

Bertina: see **Bertha**

Beryl From the jewel. Rare variant is **Berylla**. **Berry** is usual diminutive.

Berylla: see **Beryl**

Bess Independently adopted diminutive of **Elizabeth**. Main variant, **Bessie**, is in independent use.

Bessie Independently adopted diminutive of **Elizabeth** or **Bess**. Spelling variant, **Bessy**, also exists.

Bessy: see **Bessie**

Bet Independently adopted diminutive of **Elizabeth** (or **Beth**). **Bess** and **Bessie** are directly related names.

Beth Independently adopted diminutive of **Elizabeth**. Variant, **Bet**, is in independent use. Name often combines as second element of compound name to form **Jo Beth, Mary Beth**, etc., as for actresses Jo Beth Williams (born 1953) and Mary Beth Hurt (born 1948).

Betsey: see **Betsy**

Betsy: Independently adopted diminutive of **Elizabeth** (blending **Bet** or **Beth** and **Bess** or **Bessie**). Variant spelling,

Betsey, occurs, as for Betsey Trotwood, David's great-aunt in Dickens novel *David Copperfield* (1850).

Bette: see **Betty**

Bettina: see **Betty** and **Elizabeth**

Betty Independently adopted diminutive of **Elizabeth**. Variants include French form **Bette**, adopted by U.S. actress Bette Davis (1908–1989) and entertainer/actress Bette Midler (born 1944). The Italian version, **Bettina**, exists as for sociologist Bettina Aptheker (born 1944).

Beulah Biblical name (of place, not person), from Hebrew *be'ūlāh*, "she who is married." No regular variants or diminutives.

Bev: see **Beverly**

Beverley: see **Beverly**

Beverly From English surname, itself from place-name Beverley, Yorkshire, which gave male name **Beverley**. Variant spelling, **Beverley**, also widely found. Most common diminutive is **Bev**.

Bianca From Italian *bianca*, "white," itself a translation (like French **Blanche**) of Latin name **Candida**. No regular variants.

Biddy Independently adopted diminutive of **Bridget**. No regular variants.

Billie Either adoption of male name **Billie** (diminutive of **William**), intended as feminine equivalent, or as diminutive of same name when in (rare) female use. Few regular variants, but found in compounds, as for tennis player Billie Jean King (born 1943).

Bina: see **Sabina**

Binnie: see **Bernice**

Birgit: see **Bridget**

Blanche From French *blanche*, "white," itself a translation of Latin name **Candida**, familiar as saint's name. Italian variant, **Bianca**, has some vogue as an independent name.

Blodwen Welsh name, comprising *blodau*, "flowers," and *gwen*, "white," itself said to be translation of French name *Blanchefleur*. **Blodwyn** is occasional variant spelling.

Blodwyn: see **Blodwen**

Blondie From nickname for fair-haired person. Few regular variants.

Blossom From the general word, implying "flower." Few regular variants.

Blythe Either from surname or with direct reference to "blithe," meaning "happy" or "carefree." No regular variants.

Bobbie Independently adopted diminutive of **Roberta**, or (less often), **Barbara**, also regarded as feminine equivalent to male name **Bobby.** No regular variants.

Bonita Feminine form of Spanish *bonito*, "pretty," but not found as a Spanish name. Diminutive variant is **Bonny** (although this usually has a different origin).

Bonnie From Scottish word meaning "pretty" or "healthy-looking." Also spelled **Bonny.**

Bonny: see **Bonnie**

Branwen: see **Bronwen**

Bren: see **Brenda**

Brenda Perhaps ultimately from Old Norse *brandr,* "sword" (which also gave standard English "brand"). Felt by some to be feminine of Celtic name **Brendan.** Most common variant is diminutive, **Bren.**

Bride: see **Bridget**

Bridget English form of *Brighid,* name of ancient Celtic fire goddess, itself probably derived from Celtic *brigh,* "strength." Variants of name have been promoted by well-known bearers: **Brigitte** by French film star Brigitte Bardot (born 1933), **Britt** by Swedish movie actress Britt Ekland (born 1942), and **Brigid** by British novelist Brigid Brophy (born 1929). Other variants include German **Birgit,** Scandinavian **Brigitta,** and diminutives, **Bride, Bridie,** and **Gita.** Diminutive, **Biddy,** is in independent use.

Bridie: see **Bridget**

Brigid: see **Bridget**

Brigitta: see **Bridget**

Brigitte: see **Bridget**

Briony: see **Bryony**

Britt: see **Bridget**

Bron: see **Bronwen**

Bronwen Welsh name, comprising *bron,* "breast," and *gwen,* "white": "fair-bosomed." Variant is **Branwen,** but this is really a different Welsh name, meaning "beautiful raven," from *bran,* "raven," and *gwen,* "fair." True variants are **Bronwyn,** and diminutive, **Bron.**

Bronwyn: see **Bronwen**

Brook: see **Brooke**

Brooke Surname used as first name. Variant spelling is **Brook**, and expected diminutive is **Brookie**.

Brookie: see **Brooke**

Bryony From the flower (a wild climbing plant). Variant is **Briony**.

Bunny Either independently adopted diminutive of **Bernice** or from "bunny," child's nickname for rabbit. No regular variants.

Bunty Probably from nursery rhyme or lullaby about "baby bunting." No regular variants.

Caddy: see **Candace**

Caitlin: see **Catherine**

Cam: see **Camilla**

Camilla Feminine of Roman clan name *Camillus*, perhaps meaning "attendant at a sacrifice." Main variant is French spelling **Camille**. Other variants include **Cam, Cammie, Millie,** and **Milly.**

Camille: see **Camilla**

Cammie: see **Camilla**

Candace Despite modern associations with "candid" and "candy," origin and meaning of name are uncertain. In Roman era B.C., name was borne by queens of Ethiopia, one of whom is mentioned in the Bible. Name was formerly pronounced in three syllables, "Can-day-see," but now usually two, "Candiss." Spelling variant is **Candice**, as for actress Candice Bergen (born 1946). Diminutives are **Caddy** and **Candy**, with the latter in independent use.

Candi: see **Candy**

Candice: see **Candace**

Candida From Latin *candida*, "white," feminine of *Candidus*, found as Roman name, and in meaning equivalent to French name **Blanche**. Best-known variants are **Candie** and **Candy**, with the latter in independent use.

Candie: see **Candida**

Candy Either independent adoption of diminutive variant of **Candace** or **Candida**, or else directly from word "candy." Main variant is **Candi**.

Cara From Latin (or Italian) *cara*, "dear," or Irish *cara*, "friend" or "dear one." Few regular variants exist, although **Carrie** can evolve and is a name in its own right.

Carla Feminine form of **Carl**. Main variant is **Carly**, now in independent use. Alternate spelling, **Karla**, occasionally occurs, as for singer Karla Bonoff (born 1952).

Carly Either independent variant of **Carla** or feminine form of **Carl**. No regular variants.

Carmel From Mount Carmel, Israel, familiar from the Bible as a sacred place (name means "vineyard") and as twelfth-century founding site of monastic community on which order of Carmelite nuns was later based. Variants are mainly embroidered versions of name, such as **Carmelina**, **Carmelita**, and **Carmencita**.

Carmelina: see **Carmel**

Carmelita: see **Carmel**

Carmen Properly Spanish form of **Carmel**, but popularly derived from Latin *carmen*, "song." No regular variants.

Carmencita: see **Carmel**

Carol Independently adopted variant of **Caroline** (or Carolina), now often associated with Christmas songs (i.e., carols). Compare to male name **Carol**. Variants include **Carola**, as for English writer Carola Oman (1897–1978), **Carole**, as for actress Carole Lombard (1908–1942) (original name Jane Peters) and singer Carole King (born 1942), **Carroll**, and **Caryl**.

Carola: see **Carol**

Carole: see **Carol**

Caroline Originally Italian feminine form (*Carolina*) of Carlo (**Charles**). Variants include **Carolyn**, as for actress Carolyn Jones (1929–1983), and **Carolyne**. Diminutives, **Carrie** and **Lynn**, are in independent use.

Carolyn: see **Caroline**

Carolyne: see **Caroline**

Caron Welsh name, probably based on *caru*, "to love," but now felt to be related to **Carol** or **Karen**. No regular variants.

Carri: see **Carrie**

Carrie Independently adopted diminutive of **Caroline**. Two variants are **Carri** and **Carry**, with the latter familiar from American temperance reformer Carry Nation (1846–1911). Also links to form compound names such as **Carrie-Ann**.

Carrie-Ann: see **Carrie**

Carroll: see **Carol**

Carry: see **Carrie**

Caryl: see **Carol**

Cass: see **Cassandra**

Cassandra From Greek name, itself probably related to **Alexander** and meaning "ensnaring men." Common diminutive variants are **Cass**, **Cassie**, **Cassy**, and also now **Sandra**, in independent use.

Cassie: see **Cassandra**

Cassy: see **Cassandra**

Catarina: see **Catherine**

Catharine: see **Catherine**

Catherine Ultimately from Greek name *Aikaterina*, of uncertain meaning. At first linked with *aikia*, "torture," referring to St. Catherine of Alexandria, fourth-century saint (of doubtful authenticity), tortured on spiked wheel, called the "Catherine wheel," but later associated with Greek *katharos*, "pure." Spelling of this partly accounts for early versions of name such as Katharine. Vast number of variants, mainly alternating initial K- with C-, and middle vowel "e" with "a," giving **Katharine**, **Katherine**, and **Catharine.** Also quite common are such names as "continental" **Katarina** and **Catarina**, which themselves give **Katrina** and **Catrina.** Scottish variant, **Catriona**, is in independent use, as is distinctive **Kathryn.** Other forms have "l" for "r" to give such as **Kathleen** and **Cathleen**, both variants of Irish **Caitlin.** Danish form of name, **Karen**, has won independent use, as have diminutives, **Kate, Kay**, and **Kitty.** Further diminutives are **Cathy** and **Kathy.**

Cathy: see **Catherine**

Catrina: see **Catherine** and **Catriona**

Catriona Scottish variant of **Catherine** in independent use, usually pronounced "Catreena." Spelling, **Catrina**, sometimes found.

Cecil: see **Cecilia**

Cecile: see **Cecilia**

Cecilia From Latin *Caecilia*, feminine form of *Caecilius*, which gave **Cecil**. Best-known variant is **Cecily**, now in independent use. French **Cecile** and even rare **Cecil** also exist. Diminutive, **Sissy**, is in independent use.

Cecily English variant of Latin-style **Cecilia**. Most common variant spelling is **Cicely**, adopted independently. Diminutive, **Sissy**, is also in independent use.

Celeste English female adoption of French male name *Céleste*, itself from Latin name *Caelestis*, "heavenly." Few, if any, regular variants exist.

Celia From Latin *Caelia*, feminine of Roman clan name *Caelius*, itself said to derive from *caelum*, "heaven." Few established variants.

Ceri Either short form of Welsh name **Ceridwen**, or as term of affection based on Welsh *caru*, "to love." No regular variants.

Ceridwen Welsh name, comprising *cerdd*, "poetry," and *gwen*, "white" or "fair" (as for **Gwen**): "poetic goddess," or more loosely, "beautiful enough to be written about in a poem." Diminutive variant, **Ceri**, is now independent name.

Chantal French name, from Old Provençal word *cantal*, "stone" or "rock," but doubtlessly associated by English (and even French) speakers with *chant*, "song," so equated to **Carmen**. No regular variants.

Charity From the Christian virtues, like **Faith** and **Hope**. No regular variants.

Charleen: see **Charlene**

Charlene Modern feminine form of **Charles**. Variants are

Charleen, Charline, Charley, Charlie, and Charly, with the latter having "androgynous" associations in the 1980s.

Charley: see **Charlene** and **Charlotte**

Charlie: see **Charlene** and **Charlotte**

Charline: see **Charlene**

Charlotte French form of Italian *Carlotta*, itself feminine of *Carlo* (**Charles**). Many variants include **Charley, Charlie**, as in British musical *Charlie Girl* (1965), and **Charly** as for country singer Charly McClain (born 1956); see also **Charlene, Lottie, Lotty, Tottie**, and **Totty**.

Charly: see **Charlene** and **Charlotte**

Charmain: see **Charmaine**

Charmaine Probably alteration of **Charmian**, influenced by ordinary word "charm," and names such as **Lorraine**. Variant spellings include **Sharmain** and **Sharmaine**. Earlier spelling of name was often **Charmain**.

Charmian Ultimately from Greek *kharma*, "joy." Now often associated (or confused) with **Charmaine**. Suggestion of English "charm" behind name is pleasant but etymologically incorrect. No regular variants.

Cher From French *chère*, "dear," although spelling of name implies masculine of this, *cher*. No regular variants.

Cherie From French *chérie*, "dear one." Now regarded as belonging to "family" of names, **Cher, Cherry**, and **Cheryl**. Few regular variants, although spellings with "Sh-" exist, such as **Sheree, Sheri, Sherie**, and **Sherry** (adopted in own right).

Cherill: see **Cheryl**

Cherilyn: see **Cheryl**

Cherry Originally independently adopted diminutive of **Charity**, but now regarded either as a variant of names such as **Cherie** or **Cheryl**, or as a flower name, like **May** and **Rose.** No regular variants.

Cherrylyn: see **Cheryl**

Cheryl Apparently a variant of **Cherry**, influenced by **Beryl**. Also associated with French **Cherie** (pronounced with initial "Sh-"). Many spelling variants include **Cheryll**, **Cherill**, **Sheryl**, and **Sherill**, and link with **Lynn** to produce **Cherilyn** (as for singer **Cher**), **Cherrylyn**, and **Sherilyn**.

Cheryll: see **Cheryl**

Chloe Biblical name, from Greek name and word that means "young green shoot." Usual diminutive variant is simply **Clo.**

Clo: see **Chloe**

Chris Independently adopted diminutive of **Christine** and other names beginning *Chris-*. Compare to male name **Chris**. Usual diminutive is **Chrissie**, as for singer Chrissie Hynde (born 1952).

Chrissie: see **Chris**

Christabel Compound of "Christ" and Latin *bella,* "beautiful," intended to mean "fair follower of Christ." Variants include **Christabella**, and **Christobel**, with diminutives from each half as **Chris** (in independent use), **Christie**, **Bella**, and **Belle** (with the latter two now independent names).

Christabella: see **Christabel**

Christiana Early feminine form of male name **Christian**. Diminutives are **Chris** and **Christie,** with the former in independent use.

Christie: see **Christabel** and **Christiana**

Christina Shortened form of **Christiana**. Diminutive variants, **Chris, Kirsty,** and **Tina,** are in independent use.

Christine French form of **Christina**. Scandinavian form of name, **Kirsten,** is used independently, as are Scottish form, **Kirsty,** and regular diminutive, **Chris.**

Christobel: see **Christabel**

Chrystal: see **Crystal**

Cicely Independently adopted variant spelling of **Cecily**. Variants and diminutives are as for **Cecily**.

Cilla Independently adopted diminutive of **Priscilla**. No established variants. Usual diminutive suffix -*y* would produce "silly."

Cindy Independently adopted diminutive of names such as **Cynthia** and **Lucinda,** now sometimes wrongly associated with heroine of fairy tale *Cinderella* (whose name actually represents French *Cendrillon,* "little cinders"). Variants include **Cyndi,** as for singer Cyndi Lauper (born 1953), and **Sindy.**

Cissie Independently adopted diminutive of **Cecilia, Cecily,** or **Cicely**. Alternate spellings, **Cissy** and **Sissy,** occur, former as for soul singer Cissy Houston (born 1932), latter as for actress Sissy Spacek (born 1950).

Cissy: see **Cissie**

Clair: see **Claire**

Claire French form of Latin name **Clara**, which gave English **Clare**. Occasional spelling variant is **Clair**.

Clair: see **Claire**

Clara Relatinized form of English **Clare**, also representing Spanish *clara*, "clear" or "pure." Directly related variant is **Claire**, in independent use.

Clare From Latin *clara*, feminine of *clarus*, "clear," "bright," or "famous," which also gave **Clara**. Closely related to French variant, **Claire**, now in independent use.

Claribel Probably blend of **Clara** and names such as **Annabel** or **Isabel**, influenced by French *bel*, "beautiful." No regular variants.

Clarice English and French form of Latin name *Claritia*, itself probably based on *clara* (which in turn gave English **Clara**). Latinate variant of name, **Clarissa**, was adopted independently.

Clarinda Independently adopted blend of **Clare** and *-inda* ending of name such as **Belinda**. No regular variants.

Claris: see **Clarissa**

Clarissa Latinized form of **Clarice**. Variants are **Claris** and **Clarry**.

Clarry: see **Clarissa**

Claude: see **Claudia**

Claudette: see **Claudia**

Claudia Biblical name, feminine of Roman clan name *Claudius*, itself giving male name **Claude**. Variants include French **Claudine**, **Claude**, and **Claudette**, with the latter born by French actress Claudette Colbert (born 1905).

Claudine: see **Claudia**

Clem: see **Clementina**

Clementina Feminine form of **Clement**. Main variant is **Clementine**, in independent use, as is diminutive, **Cleo**. Other diminutives are **Clem**, **Clemmie**, and **Clemmy**.

Clementine Feminine form of **Clement**, with French diminutive suffix *-ine*. Directly related to **Clementina**, with same diminutives as that name.

Clemmie: see **Clementina**

Clemmy: see **Clementina**

Cleo Independently adopted diminutive of **Clementina**, **Clementine**, or **Cleopatra**. No regular variants.

Cleopatra From Greek name meaning "father's glory." Diminutive variant, **Cleo**, is in independent use.

Clo: see **Chloe** and **Clodagh**

Clodagh From name of Irish river in Co. Tipperary, but perhaps felt by some to be associated with **Claudia**. Popular diminutive is **Clo**, normally associated with **Chloe**.

Coleen: see **Colleen**

Colene: see **Colleen**

Colleen From Irish *cailín*, "girl," but felt by some to be feminine form of male name **Colin**. Variant spellings include **Coleen** and **Colene**.

Con: see **Connie**

Connie Independently adopted diminutive of **Constance**. Diminutive variant, **Con**, sometimes found.

Constance English form of Late Latin name *Constantia*, "constancy" or "perseverance." Best-known variant is **Connie**, now in independent use.

Cora From Greek *korē*, "girl" or "daughter." French variants are more popular now, especially **Corinne**, in independent use, and to a lesser extent, **Coralie**.

Coral From ordinary word, regarded as jewel name, but doubtless felt by some to be related to **Cora**. Occasional variant is **Cory**.

Coralie: see **Cora**

Cordelia Perhaps ultimately from Celtic saint's name Cordula, itself associated with Latin *cor*, genitive *cordis*, "heart." Variants include **Cordy** and **Delia**, with the latter now being an independent name (usually with a different origin).

Cordy: see **Cordelia**

Corinne French name, ultimately from same Greek source that gave **Cora**. No regular variants.

Cornelia Feminine form of Latin (now also English) name **Cornelius**. Variants include **Cornie**, **Corrie**, and **Nellie** (though the latter is now more often linked with **Nell**).

Cornie: see **Cornelia**

Corrie: see **Cornelia**

Cory: see **Coral**

Crystal From ordinary word for clear, shiny mineral or cut glass. Variant spelling is **Chrystal**, perhaps influenced by **Christine.**

Cybill: see **Sybil**

Cyndi: see **Cindy**

Cynthia From Greek name *Kynthia*, byname of Artemis, goddess of the hunt and moon, said to have been born on Mount Kynthos (Cynthus) on island of Delos. Mountain name itself is of uncertain, pre-Greek origin. Best-known variant is **Cindy**, now an independent name.

Daff: see **Daphne**

Daffy: see **Daphne**

Dahlia From the flower. Spelling variant, **Dalia**, occasionally found.

Daisy From the flower. Conventionally regarded as pet form of **Margaret**, as French equivalent of this, **Marguerite**, is French word for "daisy," so that English name may have been seen as its "translation." No regular variants.

Dale Female adoption of male name **Dale**. No established variants.

Dalia: see **Dahlia**

Dan: see **Danielle**

Dana Adopted from male name **Dana**, but popularly regarded as variant of **Danielle** or **Donna**. No regular variants.

Dandy From standard word, with perhaps suggestion of **Danny** (diminutive of **Danielle**) or even of "dainty." No established variants.

Daniela: see **Danielle**

Daniella: see **Danielle**

Danielle French feminine form of **Daniel**. Variants include

Daniela and **Daniella.** Diminutives are usually **Dan, Dannie,** and **Danny.**

Dannie: see **Danielle**

Danny: see **Danielle**

Daph: see **Daphne**

Daphne From Greek word for "laurel," with Daphne a nymph who, chased by Apollo, turned into this bush. Diminutive variants include **Daff, Daffy,** and **Daph,** with these happening to suggest "daffodil" (itself only rarely used as flower name).

Darcey Female adoption of male name **Darcy.** Few regular variants.

Darleen: see **Darlene**

Darlene Apparently based on "darling" with ending from name such as **Charlene.** Spelling variants, **Darleen** and **Darline,** occur, former as for actress of 1960s and 70s, Darleen Carr.

Darline: see **Darlene**

Daryl Female adoption of male name **Daryl** (or **Darrell**), probably influenced by name such as **Cheryl.** No regular variants.

Davena: see **Davina**

Davida: see **Davina**

Davina Scottish feminine form of **David.** Variants include **Davida, Davena,** and **Davinia,** with Davida having diminutive, **Vida.**

Davinia: see **Davina**

Dawn From ordinary word, perhaps felt to be English translation of Roman name **Aurora**. Few regular variants.

Deanna Variant of **Diana**, influenced by **Anna**. No regular variants.

Debbie Independently adopted diminutive of **Deborah**, perhaps to some suggesting "debutante," or colloquial abbreviation of this, "deb." Variant spelling, **Debby,** exists. Main diminutive is **Debs**.

Debby: see **Debbie**

Deborah Biblical name, from Hebrew *Debōrāh*, "bee" (compare to **Melissa**). Increasingly popular variant is **Debra**, as for actress Debra Winger (born 1955). Best-known diminutive is independently adopted **Debbie**.

Debra: see **Deborah**

Debs: see **Debbie**

Dee: see **Delia**

Deidre: see **Deirdre**

Deirdre From name of legendary Irish heroine, perhaps related to Irish *deardan*, "storm." To English speakers happens to suggest "dear." Variant spellings are **Deidre** and **Diedre**.

Delia Classical name, itself from Greek island of Delos, (in Greek mythology) home of Artemis and Apollo. Occasional variants include **Della** (found in own right) and **Dee**. Name is itself also a diminutive of **Cordelia**.

Delilah Biblical name, from Hebrew *Delīlāh*, "delight," although some derive it from Arabic *dalla*, "to tease" or "to flirt." No regular variants.

Dell: see **Della**

Della Independent adoption of diminutive of **Adela** or alteration of **Delia**. Usual variant is diminutive, **Dell**.

Delphina: see **Delphine**

Delphine French name, from Latin *Delphina*, "woman of Delphi." Perhaps associated by some with "delphinium" as kind of flower name. Best-known variant is **Delphina**, but **Delvene** is also found.

Delvene: see **Delphine**

Demelza Cornish name in select English-speaking use from 1950s, mainly in the U.K.

Deniece: see **Denise**

Denise French feminine form of **Dennis**. Variants include **Deneice** and **Deniece**, with the latter popularized by singer Deniece Williams (born 1951).

Dervla Irish name, perhaps meaning "daughter of a poet," from prefix *dear-*, "daughter," and *file*, "poet," or else "daughter of Ireland," from *Fál*, poetic name for Ireland. No regular variants.

Detta: see **Bernadette**

Di: see **Diana** and **Dinah**

Diahann: see **Diane**

Diana From name of Greek goddess of the moon and hunt, itself probably related to Latin *deus*, "god," and so to modern English "divine." Variants in independent use include **Deanna** and **Diane**. Usual diminutive is **Di**.

Diane French form of **Diana**. Alternate spellings, **Dianne**, **Dyan**, as for actress Dyan Cannon (born 1938), and **Diahann**, as for singer/actress Diahann Carroll (born 1935) (original name Carol Diahann Johnson), exist.

Dianne: see **Diane**

Diedre: see **Deirdre**

Dil: see **Dilys**

Dill: see **Dilys**

Dilly: see **Dilys**

Dilys Welsh name, from standard word meaning "genuine" or "sincere." Variants are mainly of spelling, as **Dylis** and **Dyllis**, with fairly common diminutives, **Dil**, **Dill**, and **Dilly**, in use.

Dina: see **Dinah**

Dinah Biblical name, from Hebrew *Dīnāh*, "vindicated." Now often associated with **Diana**, but that is a different name. Variants include **Dina** (so spelled in Puritan times) and **Di**.

Dione: see **Dionne**

Dionna: see **Dionne**

Dionne Feminine form of **Dion**. Variants include rare **Dionna** and **Dione**.

Divina Probably variant of **Davina**, influenced by "divine." One variant is **Divinia**.

Divinia: see **Divina**

Dodie: see **Dorothy**

Dodo: see **Dorothy**

Doll: see **Dolly** and **Dorothy**

Dolly Independently adopted variant of **Dorothy**. Popularly associated with "doll" (with this word itself also probably from Dorothy). Most common diminutive is **Doll**, borne by Doll Tearsheet, Falstaff's mistress in Shakespearean play *Henry IV, Part 2* (1600).

Dolores From Spanish *dolores*, "sorrows," as last word of title of Virgin Mary, *Maria de los Dolores*, "Mary of the Sorrows." **Lolita**, probably the best-known variant, became an independent name, as did **Lola**.

Dominique French feminine form of **Dominic**. Too recent to have regular variants or diminutives.

Donna From Italian word for "lady" (in Italian a title, not a name). Today correctly associated with **Madonna**. No regular variants, although name is often used in combination, especially **Donna-Marie**, which links title of Virgin Mary with her name.

Donna-Marie: see **Donna**

Dora Independently adopted short form of names such as **Dorothea**, **Theodora**, and **Isadora**. Variants include **Dorry** and **Dory**.

Dorcas From Greek word *dorkas*, "doe" or "gazelle." At first not actual name, but used in the Bible to "interpret" name **Tabitha**. No regular variants.

Doreen Probably blend of names such as **Dora**, **Dorothy**,

Kathleen (a form of **Catherine**), and **Maureen**. No regular variants.

Dorinda Blend of **Dora** and ending of name such as **Belinda**. No regular variants.

Doris From Greek name, meaning "woman from Doris" (region of central Greece), born in mythology by the mother of Nereids (i.e., sea nymphs). Later taken to be blend of names such as **Dorothy** and **Phyllis**. No regular variants.

Dorothea Earlier form of **Dorothy**, from Latin form of Greek name combining *dōron*, "gift," and *theos*, "god": (in Christian terms) "gift of God." (Greek words are reversed in male name **Theodore**.) Diminutive variants are mostly as for **Dorothy**.

Dorothy Usual English form of **Dorothea**. Variants include **Dodo**, **Doll**, **Dolly** (now used independently), **Dot**, **Dotty**, and **Dodie**.

Dorry: see **Dora**

Dory: see **Dora**

Dosia: see **Theodosia**

Dot: see **Dorothy**

Dotty: see **Dorothy**

Drucilla: see **Drusilla**

Druscilla: see **Drusilla**

Drusilla Biblical name, diminutive of Roman clan name *Drusus*, itself said to be related to Greek *drosos*, "dew": "fruitful." Variants are mainly of spellings, such as **Drucilla**

and **Druscilla**, with occasional diminutive, **Cilla**, now an independent name.

Dulce: see **Dulcie**

Dulcie Ultimately from Latin *dulcis*, "sweet." Occasional variant is **Dulce**.

Dusty Either from standard word (for pale hair or complexion), or as female form of **Dustin**. Few regular variants.

Dyan: see **Diane**

Dylis: see **Dilys**

Dyllis: see **Dilys**

Dymphna Irish name, probably a development from Gaelic name *Damhnait*, itself perhaps feminine diminutive of *damh*, "stag," or *dámh*, "poet." To non-Irish suggests blend of **Daphne** and "nymph" (logically enough, for former was latter). Main variant is **Dympna**.

Dympna: see **Dymphna**

Eartha From standard word "earth," doubtless interpreted in sense as "Mother Earth," the vital force of nature. No regular variants or diminutives.

Ebo: see **Ebony**

Ebony From word for valuable black wood. Usual diminutive is **Ebo**.

Ede: see **Edith**

Edie: see **Edith**

Edith From Old English name *Eadgȳth*, comprising *ēad*, "riches," and *gȳth*, "strife": "rich in war" or "bringing rich booty." Variant diminutives include **Ede** and **Edie**, latter as for comedienne Edie Adams (born 1929) (original name Elizabeth Edith Enke).

Edna Perhaps from Hebrew *'ēdnāh*, "rejuvenation," and related to biblical name of Garden of Eden. No established variants.

Edweena: see **Edwina**

Edwena: see **Edwina**

Edwina Feminine form of **Edwin**. Spelling variants, **Edweena** and **Edwena**, are sometimes found.

Effie Independently adopted diminutive of **Euphemia**. No regular variants.

Eglantina: see **Eglantine**

Eglantine From the flower, poetically identified with honeysuckle. Variants include **Eglantina** (giving independently adopted **Tina**) and **Eglantyne**.

Eglantyne: see **Eglantine**

Eileen English form of Irish name *Eibhlín*, itself probably form of **Aveline**. By many felt to be related to **Elaine**, but that name has a different origin. Scottish variant, **Aileen**, also occurs with rarer spellings, **Eilene** and **Ileen**, recorded.

Eilene: see **Eileen**

Eithne Irish name, said to derive from *eithne*, "kernel," presumably in metaphorical sense "fruitful." Felt by some to be feminine form of **Aidan**, and to relate to **Edna**. Usual (English) pronunciation is "Ethny." No regular variants.

Elain: see **Elaine**

Elaine From French form of **Helen**. Few variants, except for altered spellings such as **Elain** and **Elayne**.

Elayne: see **Elaine**

Eleanor Perhaps historic French spelling of form of **Helen**, or else based on Old German *al*, "all." Spelling variant, **Elinor**, is in independent use, as are diminutives, **Ellie** and **Nell**.

Eleonora: see **Leonora** and **Lora**

Elinor Independently adopted variant of **Eleanor**. Diminutives are as for **Eleanor**.

Elisabeth: see **Elizabeth**

Elise: see **Elizabeth**

Eliza Shortened form of **Elizabeth** in independent use. Related **Liza** sometimes regarded as variant.

Elizabeth Biblical name, from Hebrew *Elīsheba*, "oath of my God" or "my God has sworn." More popular than main name are many variants, mostly national forms and diminutives. **Elisabeth** is usual spelling in continental Europe, with Spanish form, **Isabel**, in independent use in English-speaking countries. Chief of diminutives, all now also in independent use, are: **Bess, Bessie, Bet, Beth, Betsy, Betty, Eliza, Elsa, Lisa, Liza, Elsie, Lisbeth,** and **Liz**. In Scotland, **Elspeth** is also found. Continental European diminutives include **Bettina, Elsa** (in independent use), **Elise, Ilse, Lise,** and **Lisette**.

Ella Ultimately, through French, from Old German *al*, "all," as probably for **Eleanor**. Now associated with **Ellen**. Most common diminutive is **Ellie**, in independent use.

Ellen Independently adopted form of **Helen**. Variants include **Ellie** and **Nell**, both in independent use.

Ellie Independently adopted diminutive of **Eleanor, Ella, Ellen, Helen,** or other name beginning *El-*. Spelling variant, **Elly,** also occurs.

Elly: see **Ellie**

Eloisa: see **Eloise**

Eloise Probably related to male name **Louis**, through Latin form of this, **Aloysius**. Most common variant is **Eloisa**.

Elsa Independently adopted short form of German *Elisabeth* (**Elizabeth**). Sometimes regarded as variant of **Elsie**, but that is a different name. Diminutive, **Ellie,** is in independent use.

Else: see **Elsie**

Elsie Independently adopted form of **Elspie**, itself diminutive of **Elspeth**. Diminutive variant is **Else**.

Elspeth Independently adopted Scottish diminutive of **Elizabeth**. Main variant is **Elspie**, which gave independently adopted **Elsie**.

Elspie: see **Elspeth**

Elvira Spanish name of uncertain origin, but possibly from Germanic name *Alwara*, itself apparently comprising *al*, "all," and *wēr*, "true": "true to all." Few, if any, regular variants exist.

Em: see **Emily** and **Emma**

Emilia Independently adopted variant of **Amelia**. Where in regular use, variants are as for **Amelia**.

Emily From Latin name *Aemilia*, feminine of Roman clan name *Aemilius*, which also partly gave **Amelia** (and its variant, **Emilia**), and entirely gave male name **Emile**. Not related to **Emma**, despite similarity. Diminutive variants include **Em**, **Emmie**, and **Emmy**.

Emma From Old German word *ermen*, "entire," found in longer names such as **Ermintrude**. Variant diminutives are **Em**, **Emmie**, and **Emmy**, with the last of these combining to form compounds, as for country singer Emmylou Harris (born 1949).

Emmeline Apparently development from **Emma** (rather than **Emily**). Diminutive, **Emmie**, evolved, as for other names beginning *Em-*.

Emmie: see **Emily**, **Emma**, and **Emmeline**

Emmy: see **Emily** and **Emma**

Emmy: see **Emily**

Ena English form of Irish name **Eithne**. Sometimes found in variant form, **Ina**.

Enid Welsh name, from *enaid*, "soul" or "life." No regular variants.

Eppie: see **Euphemia** and **Hephzibah**

Erica Feminine form of **Eric**, perhaps now regarded by some as flower name, from *Erica*, botanical name for heather genus (compare to **Heather**). Main variant is **Erika**.

Erika: see **Erica**

Erin Irish name, from poetic name for Ireland. No regular variants.

Ermintrude From Old German name, comprising *ermen*, "entire" (seen in **Emma**), and *traut*, "beloved": "wholly loved." Gave diminutive variant, **Trudy**, still in independent use.

Erna Diminutive form of **Ernesta** or **Ernestina**, feminine equivalent of **Ernest**. Few regular variants.

Ernesta: see **Erna**

Ernesta: see **Erna**

Esmé Feminine adoption of male name **Esmé**. Felt by some to be diminutive of **Esmeralda**, but that name has a different origin. Main variant spelling is **Esmée** (with name also written without accent).

Esmée: see **Esmé**

Esmeralda From Spanish word *esmeralda*, "emerald." No regular variants, although **Esmé**, really a different name, is sometimes felt to be diminutive.

Essa: see **Esther**

Esta: see **Esther** and **Hester**

Estella: see **Estelle**

Estelle French form of **Stella**. Most common variant is **Estella**, found in Dickens novel *Great Expectations* (1861) for Miss Havisham's ward.

Esther Biblical name, perhaps ultimately from Persian word meaning "star." Diminutives include **Essa**, **Esta**, and **Etty**, with variant, **Hester**, in independent use.

Eth: see **Ethel**

Ethel From first element, meaning "noble," of Old German name such as *Ethelburga*, "noble fortress," or *Ethelgive*, "noble gift". Usual variant is diminutive, **Eth**.

Etta: see **Henrietta**

Ettie: see **Henrietta**

Etty: see **Esther** and **Henrietta**

Eudora Greek name, comprising *eu*, "good," and *dōron*, "gift": "good gift." Main diminutive, independently used **Dora**, is traditionally derived from other names.

Eugenia: see **Eugenie**

Eugenie French feminine form (properly *Eugénie*) of **Eugene**. Variant, **Eugenia**, formerly in English-speaking use. Diminutives, **Gene** and **Genie**, exist.

Eunice Biblical name, from Greek name comprising *eu,* "good," and *nikē,* "victory": "good victory." Original pronunciation was "you-*nice*-ee," with middle syllable stressed, but now always "*you*-niss," with accent on first element. Variant spelling **Unice** sometimes found.

Euphemia Greek name, comprising *eu,* "well," and *phēnai,* "to speak": "well spoken of." Most common variant is diminutive, **Effie,** in independent use. **Eppie** also occurs.

Eurydice Greek name, comprising *eurys,* "wide," and *dikē,* "right" or "justice": "wide justice," or effectively, "princess" or "queen." No regular variants, if any at all.

Eustacia Feminine form of **Eustace.** Best-known variant is diminutive, **Stacy,** now in independent use.

Eva Latin and continental European form of **Eve.** Usual diminutive is **Evie.**

Evadne Greek name, comprising *eu,* "well," and another word of uncertain origin. No regular variants.

Evalyn: see **Evelyn**

Evangeline Fancifully formed from Latin *evangelium,* "gospel," itself from Greek *euangelion,* literally "good news." Diminutive, **Eva,** is in independent use. **Evie** also exists.

Eve Biblical name, from French form of Latin *Eva,* itself from Hebrew *havvāh,* "living." Variant form, **Eva,** exists independently. Spanish diminutive form **Evita** promoted by Argentinian political leader Evita (Eva) Perón (1922–1952), and subsequent musical of same name, based on her life. Diminutive, **Evie,** also occurs.

Evelina: see **Evelyn**

Evelyn From surname, itself probably from French female name *Aveline*. Sometimes felt to be compound name, combining **Eve** (or **Eva**) and **Lynn**. See also male name **Evelyn**. Spelling variant, **Evelina**, is in use and **Evalyn** also exists, as for actress Evalyn Knapp (1908–1981). Usual diminutive is **Evie**.

Evie: see **Eva**, **Evangeline**, **Eve**, and **Evelyn**

Evita: see **Eve**

Evonne: see **Yvonne**

Fabia Ultimately from Roman clan name *Fabius*, itself from Latin *faba*, "bean." No regular variants.

Faith From ordinary word, denoting the virtues, like **Hope** and **Charity.** No regular variants, although **Faithie** is a diminutive. **Fay** is an independent name of a different origin.

Faithie: see **Faith**

Fan: see **Fannie** and **Fanny**

Fancy From the standard English word, but probably influenced also by **Fanny** and "fiancée." No regular variants.

Fannie Independently adopted variant of **Fanny.** Diminutive **Fan** sometimes found.

Fanny Independently used diminutive of **Frances.** Variant, **Fannie,** was (and may still be) in independent use. Diminutive can be **Fan.**

Fatima Arabic name, from *fāṭima*, "weaning one." No regular variants.

Fay From "fay," former English word for fairy, though sometimes associated with **Faith,** which has a different origin. Variant spelling is **Faye,** as for film actress Faye Dunaway (born 1941).

Faye: see **Fay**

Felicia: see **Felicity**

Felicity From ordinary word, denoting good fortune and luck, developing from Latin *felicitas*, "happiness." Variant, **Felicia,** was formerly quite common. Diminutive variants are **Flick** and the rare **Lucky.**

Fenella English form of Irish *Fionnguala*, meaning "white shoulder." Variants include **Finella, Nella,** and **Nula,** with the latter now in independent use.

Fern From the woodland plant with feathery fronds. No regular variants.

Fidelia From Latin *fidelis*, "faithful." No regular variants.

Finella: see **Fenella**

Fiona From Scottish Gaelic *fionn*, "white" or "fair." Few, if any, regular variants exist.

Flavia Feminine form of Roman clan name *Flavius*, itself from *flavus*, "yellow," probably referring to fair hair of original bearers. No regular variants, though diminutive, **Flavie,** sometimes found.

Flavie: see **Flavia**

Fleur From standard French word for "flower," perhaps having additional suggestion of "flirt" for some. No regular variants.

Flick: see **Felicity**

Flo: see **Floella, Florence,** and **Flora**

Floella From blend of **Flora** or **Florence** and **Ella,** with latter also found as final element in such names as **Arabella** and **Fenella.** No regular variants, although **Flo** (normally from **Flora** or **Florence**) is possible.

Flora From name of Roman goddess of flowers and of spring. Like **Florence**, has diminutive variants, **Flo**, **Florrie**, **Floss**, and **Flossie**.

Florence Form of *Florentia*, feminine of Latin name *Florentius*, itself based on *florens*, "blossoming." Variants are chiefly diminutives, such as **Florrie**, **Floss**, **Flossie**, and **Flo**.

Florrie: see **Flora** and **Florence**

Floss: see **Flora** and **Florence**

Flossie: see **Flora** and **Florence**

Fran: see **Frances**

Frances Feminine form of **Francis**, with both spellings formerly found for both sexes. Continental European variants are French **Françoise**, Italian **Francesca**, and Spanish **Francisca**, while many diminutives include **Frannie**, **Franny**, **Frankie**, and **Fran**, with French **Francine**, diminutive of Françoise, also in English-speaking use. Best-known variant, however, is **Fanny**, in independent use.

Francesca: see **Frances**

Francine: see **Frances**

Francisca: see **Frances**

Françoise: see **Frances**

Frankie: see **Frances**

Frannie: see **Frances**

Franny: see **Frances**

Fred: see **Frederica**

Freda Independently adopted diminutive of name such as **Winifred** and **Frederica**. Variant form, adopted independently, is **Frieda**.

Freddie: see **Frederica**

Frederica Feminine form of **Frederick**. Variants include French **Frédérique**, "continental" **Frederika** and **Frederike**, and diminutives, **Freddie**, **Freda** (in independent use), **Fred**, **Rickie**, **Ricky**, and **Rica**.

Frederika: see **Frederica**

Frederike: see **Frederica**

Frédérique: see **Frederica**

Freya From Norse goddess of love and fecundity, who also gave the name of the day of the week, *Friday*. Name itself is probably related to modern German *Frau*, "woman." No regular variants.

Frieda Independently adopted variant of **Freda**, with spelling influenced by German equivalent, *Friede*. Few regular variants.

Gabi: see **Gabrielle**

Gabriela: see **Gabrielle**

Gabriella: see **Gabrielle**

Gabrielle French feminine form of **Gabriel**. Variants include **Gabriela** and **Gabriella**, former as for Italian tennis player Gabriela Sabatini (born 1970). Usual diminutives are **Gabi** and **Gaby**.

Gaby: see **Gabrielle**

Gail Independently adopted diminutive of **Abigail**. Variant spellings include **Gale**, in independent use, and **Gayle**.

Gale Independently adopted variant of **Gail**, perhaps influenced by standard word "gale." Alternate spelling, **Gayle**, also occurs.

Gay From ordinary word, strictly speaking through French *gai*, "joyful." Most common variant is **Gaye**.

Gaye: see **Gay**

Gayle: see **Gail** and **Gale**

Gaynor Medieval form of **Guinevere**, thus also related to **Jennifer**. No regular variants.

Geena: see **Gina**

Gem: see **Gemma**

Gemma From Italian word for "gem" or "jewel," itself long established as a name in that country. Probably felt by some to be related to **Emma**. Variant spelling, **Jemma**, sometimes found, with **Gem** used as diminutive.

Gene Either independently adopted diminutive of **Eugenia** or respelled **Jean**. Seen by some as borrowing of male name **Gene**. Few regular variants. **Ginny** sometimes regarded as one although it usually represents **Virginia**.

Gene: see **Eugenie**

Genie: see **Eugenie**

Genevieve Said to be from Germanic words *geno*, "race" (related to English "generation"), and *wefa*, "woman" (English "wife"). Few regular variants exist, although diminutives could easily be created.

George: see **Georgette, Georgia, Georgiana,** and **Georgina**

Georgette French feminine form of **George**. Most common variants are diminutives, **Georgie** and **George**.

Georgia Standard feminine form of **George**, perhaps associated in the U.S. with state name (although that was for George II). Variants are usually **Georgie** and **George**.

Georgiana Feminine form of **George**. Main variants are **Georgie** and **Georgy**.

Georgie: see **Georgette, Georgia, Georgiana,** and **Georgina**

Georgina Feminine form of **George**. Usual variants are **Georgie, George,** and **Gina**, now in independent use.

Georgy: see **Georgiana**

Geraldine Feminine form of **Gerald**. Most common variants are diminutives **Gerrie, Gerry, Jerrie,** and **Jerry,** with the last of these familiar from model Jerry Hall (born 1956).

Gerda Probably from Old Norse *garthr,* "enclosure" or "protected place." Now sometimes felt to be feminine of **Gerard** or form of **Gertrude.** No regular variants.

Germaine French feminine form of now rare male name *Germain,* itself from late Latin *Germanus,* "brother," doubtless originally in Christian context. Variant spelling, **Jermaine,** exists.

Gerrie: see **Geraldine**

Gerry: see **Geraldine**

Gert: see **Gertrude**

Gertie: see **Gertrude**

Gertrude From Old German name comprising *gār,* "spear," and *traut,* "strength": "strong with (or as) the spear." Best-known variants are diminutives **Gert, Gertie, Trudie,** and **Trudy,** with the last of these in independent use.

Ghislaine From Old French form of **Giselle.** Usual pronunciation is "Gizz-lane," with hard "G" as in "give." Diminutive, **Gigi,** occurs.

Gigi: see **Ghislaine**

Gilda Apparently Italian diminutive form of Old German name known to Anglo-Saxons as *Eormenhild,* with *hild* meaning "sacrifice." No regular variants.

Gill: see **Gillian**

Gillian Either feminine form of **Julian,** or alternate independent form of **Juliana.** Variants include spelling variant, **Jillian**, and diminutives **Gill**, **Gillie**, and **Gilly**. **Jill**, originally also diminutive, is now in independent use.

Gillie: see **Gillian**

Gilly: see **Gillian**

Gina Independently adopted diminutive of **Georgina**. Variant spelling, **Geena**, sometimes occurs.

Ginevra Italian form of **Guinevere**, adopted independently. Usual variants are diminutives **Ginnie** and **Ginny**.

Ginger Either independently adopted diminutive of **Virginia**, or as descriptive name given to baby with red hair. Most common variant is diminutive, **Ginny**, as for **Virginia** itself.

Ginnie: see **Ginevra**

Ginny: see **Gene**, **Ginevra**, **Ginger**, and **Virginia**

Gipsy: see **Gypsy**

Gisele: see **Giselle**

Giselle French name, itself of Germanic origin, with *gisil* meaning "pledge" (modern German *Geisel* is word for "hostage"). Usually pronounced in French way, with soft "G," and "s" as "z." Suggestion of "gazelle" may have assisted adoption. Variant spelling, **Gisele**, sometimes found.

Gita: see **Bridget**

Glad: see **Gladys**

Gladdie: see **Gladys**

Gladdy: see **Gladys**

Gladys English form of Welsh name *Gwladys*, itself perhaps feminine form of *gwledig*, "ruler," or else a form of **Claudia**. Chance association with English "glad" is advantageous. Most common variants are diminutives **Glad**, **Gladdie**, and **Gladdy**.

Glen: see **Glenda**, **Glenn**, and **Glenys**

Glenda Modern Welsh name, comprising *glân*, "clean" or "pure," and *da*, "good," but perhaps also half-suggested by fifteenth-century Welsh rebel chieftain Owen Glendower (*Owain Glyndŵr*). Most common variant is diminutive, **Glen**, suggesting (false) association with word "glen" or male name **Glen**.

Glenn Either from male name **Glenn** or as diminutive form of **Glenda** or **Glenys**. No regular variants, although **Glen** is a logical development.

Glenys Welsh name, probably independent variant of **Glynis** but could also be blend of **Gladys** and **Glenda**. Most usual variant is diminutive **Glen**.

Gloria Direct borrowing of Latin *gloria*, "glory," doubtlessly partly prompted by earlier name *Gloriana*, poetic epithet for Queen Elizabeth I. Best-known variant is **Glory**.

Glory: see **Gloria**

Glyn: see **Glynis**

Glynis Welsh name, perhaps alteration of **Gladys** influenced by *glyn*, "valley." Spelling variant, **Glynnis**, exists, as for actress Glynnis O'Connor (born 1956). **Glenys** is an independent name. Usual diminutive is **Glyn**.

Glynnis: see **Glynis**

Golda: see **Goldie**

Goldie From word "gold," usually with reference to fair hair. Has prime form **Golda**, as for Israeli prime minister Golda Meir (1898–1978). See also **Marigold**.

Grace From ordinary word, denoting virtue. Usual diminutive is **Gracie**, promoted by comedienne Gracie Allen (1902–1964).

Gracie: see **Grace**

Greer From Scottish surname, itself form of Gregor (**Gregory**). No established variants.

Greta Independently adopted diminutive of *Margareta*, Swedish form of **Margaret**. No regular variants.

Gretchen German diminutive form of *Margarete* (**Margaret**), with -*chen* denoting as "little" (as in *Mädchen*, "girl"). No regular variants.

Griselda Probably Germanic name in origin, comprising *gris*, "gray," and *hild*, "battle." It has been associated with modern English "grizzle," but this word's origin is unknown. Variant is diminutive, **Zelda**, found in independent use.

Gudrun Germanic name, with elements corresponding to Old English *gūth*, "battle," and *rūn*, "secret" (modern English "rune"): "wily in battle." No regular variants.

Guinevere French form of Old Welsh name *Gwenhwyfar*, comprising *gwen*, "white" or "fair," and *hwyfar*, "smooth" or "soft," so perhaps means "with soft fair hair" or "with smooth fair skin" (or even with both). No regular variants. **Gaynor** is a form of name.

Gus: see **Augusta**

Gussie: see **Augusta**

Gwen Welsh name, either independently adopted diminutive of **Gwendolen** or **Gwyneth**, or direct from *gwen*, feminine form of *gwyn*, "white" or "fair." No regular variants.

Gwenda Welsh name, comprising *gwen*, "white" or "fair," and *da*, "good." No regular variants.

Gwendolen Welsh name, from *gwen*, "white" or "fair," and *dolen*, "ring" or "bow." Most common variant is diminutive **Gwen**, in independent use. Variant spellings, **Gwendoline** and **Gwendolyn**, are also found, doubtlessly influenced by names such as **Marilyn** and **Caroline**. Gwendoline Chickerell is the sister of central character, Ethelberta Petherwin, in Hardy novel *The Hand of Ethelberta* (1876). Gwendolyn Brooks is an American writer (born 1917).

Gwendoline: see **Gwendolen**

Gwendolyn: see **Gwendolen**

Gweneth: see **Gwyneth**

Gwenneth: see **Gwyneth**

Gwenyth: see **Gwyneth**

Gwyneth Welsh name, from *gwynaeth*, "luck" or "happiness." Sometimes associated with new Welsh county name Gwynedd, but that has a different (although ancient) origin. Variant spellings include **Gwynneth**, **Gwenyth**, **Gweneth**, and **Gwenneth**, with diminutive, **Gwen**, in independent use.

Gwynneth: see **Gwyneth**

Gypsy From ordinary word, having associations of romance, magic, and "the open road." Alternate spelling, **Gipsy**, occurs.

Haidee Perhaps from Greek word *aidoios*, "modest," though now popularly regarded as variant of **Heidi**. Few, if any, established variants exist.

Hannah Biblical name, from Hebrew *Hannāh*, "favor" or "grace," which also gave **Ann**. Variant diminutives of name include **Hannie** and **Hanny**. **Nancy** is an independently adopted variant.

Hannie: see **Hannah**

Hanny: see **Hannah**

Harrie: see **Harriet**

Harriet Feminine form of **Harry**. Variants include spelling adaptions, **Harrietta** and **Harriette**, and diminutives, **Harrie** and **Harry**. Diminutive variant, **Hattie**, is in independent use.

Harrietta: see **Harriet**

Harriette: see **Harriet**

Harry: see **Harriet**

Hat: see **Hattie**

Hattie Independently adopted diminutive of **Harriet**. Variant spelling, **Hatty**, occurs, as does diminutive, **Hat**.

Hatty: see **Hattie**

Hayley From surname. Few established variants.

Haze: see **Hazel**

Hazel From the plant, but later popularly associated with color of eyes. Irregular spelling variants exist, with **Haze** the usual diminutive.

Heather From the plant. (See also **Erica**.) No regular variants or diminutives.

Hebe Greek name, from *hēbos*, "young." No established variants.

Hedda Independently adopted diminutive of Scandinavian name *Hedvig*, itself comprising Germanic words meaning (more or less synonymously) "battle" and "war." No regular variants.

Heidi From diminutive form of German name *Adelheid* (**Adelaide**). No regular variants.

Helen English form of Greek name *Hēlēnē*, perhaps related to *hēlios*, "sun," and having the general meaning, "shining one." Many variants exist, several of which now enjoy independent use, including **Helena**, **Ella**, **Ellen**, and **Nell**.

Helena Latinized form of **Helen**. Variants exist as for **Helen**, with **Lena** gaining independent use.

Hennie: see **Henrietta**

Henny: see **Henrietta**

Henrietta English form of French *Henriette*, itself feminine diminutive form of *Henri* (**Henry**). Several diminutives exist, including: **Etta**, **Ettie**, **Etty**, **Hennie**, **Henny**, **Hettie**, **Hetty**, **Nettie**, and **Netty**.

Hephzibah Biblical name, from Hebrew *Hephtsībāh*, "in her is my delight" (i.e., in newborn daughter). Alternate spelling, **Hepzibah**, exists. Usual diminutive is **Hepsie**, but in George Eliot novel *Silas Marner* (1861) Silas' adopted daughter, Hephzibah Cass, is given nickname, **Eppie.**

Hepsie: see **Hephzibah**

Hepzibah: see **Hephzibah**

Hermia Contracted (but not diminutive) form of **Hermione.** No regular variants or diminutives.

Hermione Greek feminine form of *Hermes.* No regular variants, although **Hermia** is sometimes regarded as diminutive.

Hertha From name, ultimately meaning "strong" or "bold," of German goddess of fertility and growth also known as *Nertha* (with "N" apparently misread as "H"). No regular variants or diminutives.

Hester Independently adopted variant of **Esther.** Variants are **Esta, Hettie,** and **Hetty,** with the latter two being diminutives as well.

Hettie: see **Henrietta** and **Hester**

Hetty: see **Henrietta** and **Hester**

Hil: see **Hilary**

Hilary Feminine adoption of male name **Hilary.** Few regular variants, apart from **Hillary.** Diminutives **Hil** and **Hilly,** exist.

Hilda From first part of some German name beginning *Hild-*, such as **Hildegard**, with element meaning "battle." Most common variant is **Hylda.**

Hildegard Old German name, comprising *hild*, "battle," and *gard,* "enclosure" or "protected area": "comrade in arms." Variant spelling, **Hildegarde,** is common, while diminutive, **Hilda,** is in independent use.

Hildegarde: see **Hildegard**

Hillary: see **Hilary**

Hilly: see **Hilary**

Holly From the tree, with its colorful berries and Christmas associations. No regular variants.

Honor Either English form of Latin name *Honoria,* feminine of *Honorius,* "man of honor," or direct from ordinary word "honor." Best-known variant is **Honoria,** from which diminutive **Nora** has gained independent use.

Honoria: see **Honor**

Hope From the virtue, matching its "sisters," **Faith** and **Charity.** No regular variants.

Hortense French form of *Hortensia,* Latin feminine equivalent of *Hortensius,* Roman clan name probably based on Latin *hortus,* "garden." Most common variant is **Hortensia.** Few regular diminutives.

Hortensia: see **Hortense**

Hyacinth From the flower, but also serving as feminine adoption of identical male name **Hyacinth.** No regular variants.

Hylda: see **Hilda**

Hypatia Greek name, from *hypatos,* "highest." Few established variants exist, although **Patsy** (usually from **Patricia**) is possible.

Ianthe Greek name, from *ion*, "violet," and *anthos*, "flower." No regular variants.

Ibby: see **Isabel**

Ida Either from element of Old German name, *īd*, "work," or as shortening of *Iduna*, name of Norse goddess of youth and spring. Also associated with Mount Ida, Crete, which has classical connections. No regular variants.

Ileen: see **Eileen**

Ilse: see **Elizabeth**

Immy: see **Imogen**

Imogen Arose as misreading of *Innogen*, this in turn deriving either from Latin *innocens*, "innocent," or, more likely, from Celtic word related to Irish *inghean*, "daughter" or "girl." Suggestion of English "image" or "imagine" may attract name-givers or adopters. Variant spelling is **Imogene,** as for comedienne Imogene Coca (born 1908). Diminutive is **Immy.**

Imogene: see **Imogen**

Ina Independent use of final element of names such as **Edwina, Georgina,** and **Martina,** in same way as for **Ena,** of which it could also be a variant spelling. Few regular variants.

India From the country name. No established variants.

Indiana Either from the U.S. state or as an elaboration of **India**. No regular variants, although logical diminutive would be **Indy**.

Indy: see **Indiana**

Inga: see **Ingrid**

Inge: see **Ingrid**

Ingrid Scandinavian name, from combination of *Ing*, Norse fertility god, and either *fríthr*, "fair," or *rída*, "to ride." Variants include **Inga** and **Inge**.

Iolanthe Probably modern coinage, from Greek *iolē*, "violet," and *anthos*, "flower," perhaps influenced by name such as **Violetta**. Also linked with name **Yolande**. No regular variants.

Iona Probably from the Scottish island, where St. Columba founded monastery in sixth century, rather than from *Ionia*, ancient region of Asia Minor. Few effective variants.

Irene From Greek name *Eirene*, meaning "peace." Formerly pronounced "I-re-ne," in three syllables, but now in two. Variant is **Rene**, pronounced "Ree-nee," not to be confused with **Renée**, a different name.

Iris Probably blend of name of Greek goddess of the rainbow and the flower name. No regular variants.

Irma From first element of Old German name such as *Irmgard* (compare to **Ermintrude**), this meaning "whole." No regular variants.

Isa: see **Isabel**

Isabel Spanish form of **Elizabeth**, long used as independent name. Italian form of name, **Isabella**, is in independent use, as is variant spelling **Isobel**. Diminutives include **Bella, Ella** (now also used in own right), **Ibby, Isa, Nib, Sib,** and similar short forms.

Isabella Italian form of **Elizabeth**. Same variants and diminutives as for closely related **Isabel**. French equivalent, **Isabelle**, also found, as for young countess Isabelle de Croye in Scott novel *Quentin Durward* (1823).

Isabelle: see **Isabella**

Isadora Feminine form of **Isidore**. Most common variant is **Isidora**, which is closer to original name. Two diminutives are **Issy** and **Izzy**.

Isidora: see **Isadora**

Isla Scottish name, more likely adopted from name of island of Islay than variant of **Isabella**. No regular variants.

Isobel Variant form of **Isabel**. Diminutives are as for **Isabel**.

Isolda: see **Isolde**

Isolde From Old French name *Iseult* (*Yseult*), itself from Celtic root meaning "fair." (Welsh equivalent is *Esyllt*.) Common variant spelling is **Isolda**.

Issy: see **Isadora**

Ivy From the plant. No regular variants.

Izzy: see **Isadora**

Jacalyn: see **Jacqueline**

Jackey: see **Jackie**

Jacki: see **Jackie**

Jackie Independently adopted diminutive of **Jacqueline**. Many alternate spellings exist, including **Jackey**, **Jacki**, **Jacqui**, and **Jaquie**.

Jaclyn: see **Jacqueline**

Jacqueline French feminine diminutive of *Jacques* (**James**). Many alternate spellings exist, including **Jacalyn**, **Jaqueline**, **Jacquelyn**, and **Jaclyn**, as for actress Jaclyn Smith (born 1947). Diminutive, **Jackie**, now in independent use. **Jacquetta** is a related name.

Jacquelyn: see **Jacqueline**

Jacquetta Like **Jacqueline**, a French feminine diminutive of *Jacques* (**James**). Variant, **Jaquenetta**, now rare, is name of "a country wench" in Shakespeare play *Love's Labour's Lost* (1598). Diminutives are mostly as for **Jacqueline**.

Jacqui: see **Jackie**

Jade From the semi-precious stone. No regular variants.

Jaime: see **Jamie**

Jamie Female adoption of male name **Jamie**, used as equivalent for **James**. Variant spelling, **Jaime**, exists.

Jan Either independently adopted diminutive of **Janet** or **Janice**, feminine equivalent of **John**, or simple alternative to **Jane**, **Jean**, and **Joan**. No regular variants.

Jancis Apparently blend of **Jane** and either **Frances** or **Cicely**. No regular variants.

Jane English form of Latin *Johanna*, itself feminine form of *Johannes* (**John**). **Janet**, **Janice**, **Jennie**, and **Jenny** are directly related names. Spelling variant, **Jayne**, is used in own right. Diminutives include **Janie** and **Janey**. Name is often added to another to form compounds, such as **Mary Jane** and **Sarah Jane** (sometimes with hyphen).

Janet Independently adopted diminutive of **Jane**. Bearers of name have long been called **Jess** or **Jessie** in Scotland. Diminutives, **Jennie**, **Jenny**, and **Netta**, are in independent use.

Janey: see **Jane**

Janice Independently adopted diminutive of **Jane**, with *-ice* from names such as **Bernice** and **Candice**. Common variant spelling is **Janis**, in independent use.

Janie: see **Jane**

Janine Alteration of French *Jeannine*, feminine form of *Jean* (**John**). Sometimes spelled **Jannine**. Usual diminutive is **Jan**, now an independent name.

Janis Independently adopted spelling variant of **Janice**, influenced by other names ending *-is* or *-ys*, such as **Mavis** and **Gladys**. No established variants.

Jannine: see **Janine**

Jaqueline: see **Jacqueline**

Jaquenetta: see **Jacquetta**

Jaquie: see **Jackie**

Jasmin: see **Jasmine**

Jasmine From the flower, now usually spelled "jasmin." Variant spellings are **Jasmin** and **Yasmin**, with the latter in independent use.

Jay As female name, probably independently adopted diminutive of any name beginning with *J*, as written pronunciation of this letter. See also male name **Jay**. No regular variants or diminutives.

Jayne Independently adopted variant spelling of **Jane**. **Jaynie** exists as a diminutive.

Jaynie: see **Jayne**

Jean From Old French form (*Jehane*) of Latin *Johanna*, feminine of *Johannes* (**John**). Variants include diminutives, **Jeanette** (in independent use), **Jeanie**, and **Jeannie**.

Jeanette Independently adopted French diminutive of *Jeanne* (**Jean**). Variant spelling is **Jeannette**.

Jeanie: see **Jean**

Jeannette: see **Jeanette**

Jeannie: see **Jean**

Jem: see **Jemima**

Jemima Biblical name, from Hebrew *Yĕmīmah*, "wild dove." Main variants are diminutives **Jem**, **Jemmy**, and **Mima**.

Jemma: see **Gemma**

Jemmy: see **Jemima**

Jenifer: see **Jennifer**

Jenna Latin-style form of **Jenny**. No regular variants.

Jenni: see **Jennie** and **Jenny**

Jennie Independently adopted spelling variant of **Jenny**. Alternate spelling, **Jenni**, also occurs.

Jennifer Cornish form of **Guinevere**. Variants include spelling moderation, **Jenifer**, and diminutives, **Jennie** and **Jenny**, both in independent use.

Jenny Independently adopted diminutive of **Jane**, **Janet**, and **Jennifer**. Most common variant is **Jennie**, in independent use. **Jenni** is also found.

Jermaine: see **Germaine**

Jerrie: see **Geraldine**

Jerry: see **Geraldine**

Jess: see **Janet** and **Jessie**

Jessi: see **Jessie**

Jessica Apparently introduced by Shakespeare as form of biblical name *Iscah*, itself from Hebrew meaning "God beholds." Now sometimes regarded as feminine form of **Jesse**. Variant diminutive is **Jessie**, in independent use.

Jessie Either Scottish diminutive of **Jean** or **Janet**, or independently adopted diminutive of **Jessica**. Variant spellings include **Jessi** and **Jessye**. Main diminutive is **Jess**.

Jessye: see **Jessie**

Jill Modern spelling of Gill, itself a diminutive of **Gillian**. Popular diminutives are **Jillie** and **Jilly**.

Jillian: see **Gillian**

Jillie: see **Jill**

Jilly: see **Jill**

Jo Independently adopted diminutive of **Joan, Joanna, Josephine**, or similar name. Can combine with other names to form compounds, as for actress Jo Beth Williams (born 1953).

Jo Anne: see **Joanne**

Jo Beth: see **Beth**

Joan English form of Latin *Johanna*, feminine of *Johannes* (**John**). **Joanne**, from French form of name, is in independent use, as is related name **Joanna**. See also **Jo**.

Joanna Originally biblical name, as Latin form of Greek *Iōanna*, feminine form of *Iōannes* (**John**), but later regarded as independently adopted variant of **Joan**. Variants and diminutives are as for **Joan**, with **Joanne** now regarded as a directly related name.

Joanne English adoption of Old French feminine form of *Joanne* (**John**), so equivalent of **Joan**. Now more readily associated with **Joanna**, although this really has a different origin. Frequently "split" into a compound name, **Jo Anne** (sometimes with hyphen), as if from two names, **Jo** and **Ann**.

Jocasta From Greek name of uncertain origin, but derived by some from name of mythological character *Io*, associated (in some stories) with moon, and *kaustikos*, "burning"

(English "caustic"): "shining moon." No regular variants exist, but usual diminutive is **Jo**, used independently.

Jocelin: see **Jocelyn**

Joceline: see **Jocelyn**

Jocelyn From surname, and formerly more in male than female use, as now. (See male **Jocelyn** for origin.) Now usually felt to be blend of **Joyce** and **Lynn**. Several variant spellings are in use, including **Jocelin**, **Joceline**, **Joscelin**, **Josceline**, and **Joselyn**. Common diminutive is **Joss**.

Jodie: see **Jody**

Jody Apparently alteration or diminutive of names such as **Jo**, **Josephine**, **Josie**, **Judith**, or blend formed from these. Compare to male name **Jody**. Variant spelling, **Jodie**, is familiar from actress Jodie Foster (born 1962).

Jolene Apparently blend of **Jo** and second half of name such as **Marlene**. No regular variants.

Joni Independently adopted respelling of *Joanie*, diminutive of **Joan**. No regular variants, but diminutive, **Jo**, exists, as for other names beginning "Jo-."

Joscelin: see **Jocelyn**

Josceline: see **Jocelyn**

Joselyn: see **Jocelyn**

Josephine French diminutive of *Josèphe*, feminine form of **Joseph**. Best-known derivative is diminutive, **Josie**, in independent use, but **Jo** also exists.

Josie Independent adoption of **Josephine**. Usual diminutive is independently adopted **Jo**.

Joss: see **Jocelyn**

Joy From the ordinary word. No established variants or diminutives.

Joyce Either from surname or English form of Norman male name *Josce*, ultimately of Celtic origin, meaning "lord." Commonly associated with **Joy** or ordinary words "joy" and "rejoice." Frequent diminutive is **Joy**, in independent use.

Juanita English adoption of Spanish diminutive of male name *Juan* (**John**). Few regular variants are in use, although diminutive, **Nita**, exists.

Judi: see **Judith** and **Judy**

Judith Biblical name, from Hebrew *Yĕhūdhīth*, "woman of Judea" or "Jewess." Diminutives, **Jody** and **Judy**, are now used independently. **Judi** is also found.

Judy Diminutive form of **Judith** in independent use. Fairly common variant is respelling **Judi**.

Jules: see **Julia**, **Julie**, and **Juliet**

Julia From Latin name, itself feminine form of **Julius**. French form of name, **Julie**, is in independent use. Diminutive sometimes found is **Jules**.

Juliana Feminine form of Latin name *Julianus* (**Julian**). Variants, **Julianna** and **Julianne**, occur, as does derivative compound, **Julie Ann**.

Julianna: see **Juliana**

Julianne: see **Juliana**

Julie French form of **Julia**. Diminutive, **Jules**, sometimes found.

Julie Ann: see **Juliana**

Juliet English form of Italian name *Giulietta*, itself diminutive of *Giulia* (**Julia**). French spelling, **Juliette**, also occurs, while diminutive is either **Julie**, now in independent use, or **Jules**.

Juliette: see **Juliet**

June From name of month, when spring passes into summer. No regular variants or diminutives.

Justie: see **Justine**

Justina: see **Justine**

Justine French feminine form of **Justin**. Variant, **Justina**, was former regular form, and occurs in Trollope novel *Framley Parsonage* (1861) as name of Lady Meredith's daughter. Diminutives **Justie** and **Justy** are sometimes used.

Justy: see **Justine**

Karen Independent adoption of Danish or Norwegian diminutive of **Catherine**. Variant spellings are **Karin** and **Karyn**.

Karin: see **Karen**

Karla: see **Carla**

Karyn: see **Karen**

Katarina: see **Catherine**

Kate Independently adopted diminutive of **Catherine** and **Katharina**. Common variants are **Katie** and **Katy**, both in independent use.

Kath: see **Kathryn**

Katharina: see **Kate**

Katharine: see **Catherine**

Katherine: see **Catherine**

Kathie: see **Kathryn**

Kathleen: see **Catherine**

Kathryn Independently adopted variant of **Catherine**. Diminutives, **Kath**, **Kathie**, and **Kathy**, exist.

Kathy: see **Catherine** and **Kathryn**

Katie Independently adopted diminutive of **Kate**. Spelling variant, **Katy**, is also in independent use.

Katina Modern Greek diminutive form of **Catherine**. No regular variants.

Katrina: see **Catherine**

Katy Independently adopted diminutive of **Kate**. Spelling variant, **Katie**, is also used in own right.

Kay Independently adopted diminutive of name beginning with *K*, especially **Katherine** (**Catherine**) and its variants. Most common variant is **Kaye**.

Kaye: see **Kay**

Kayleigh Perhaps development from **Kelly** or **Kylie**, influenced by **Leigh** (variant of **Lee**). Alternate spellings, **Kayley** and **Kayly**, exist, among others.

Kayley: see **Kayleigh**

Kayly: see **Kayleigh**

Kellie: see **Kelly**

Kelly From Irish surname. Came to be associated with **Kerry**, **Kyle**, and **Kylie**, especially in Australia, although the latter two have different origins. Variant spelling is **Kellie**.

Keren: see **Kerenhappuch**

Kerenhappuch Biblical name, from Hebrew, meaning "horn of antimony" (used as eyelash dye in ancient times). Usual diminutive is **Keren**, completely unrelated to **Karen**.

Keri: see **Kerry**

Kerrie: see **Kerry**

Kerry Of Australian origin, and probably alteration of **Kelly**.

Was originally male name (see **Kerry**). Also spelled **Kerrie**, **Keri**, and **Kiri**.

Kezia: see **Keziah**

Keziah Biblical name, from Hebrew *Qětsī'āh*, "cassia" (name of tree yielding cinnamon; English word evolved from Hebrew). Alternate spelling is **Kezia**, while common diminutive is **Kizzie**.

Kim Independently adopted diminutive of male name **Kimberley**, and like it also originally masculine (see male name **Kim**). Now, however, usually regarded as a diminutive of female name **Kimberley**. Diminutives, **Kimmie** and **Kimmy**, are sometimes found.

Kimberley Adoption of male name **Kimberley** (which has its own origin in male names section). Variant spelling, **Kimberly**, is preferred in the U.S. Obvious diminutive is **Kim**, although this originated as diminutive of male name. **Kimmie** and **Kimmy** are also used.

Kimberly: see **Kimberley**

Kimmie: see **Kim** and **Kimberley**

Kimmy: see **Kim** and **Kimberley**

Kiri: see **Kerry**

Kirsteen: see **Kirsten**

Kirsten Danish or Norwegian form of **Christine**. Common variant spellings are **Kirsteen** and **Kirstin**. Diminutive is usually **Kirsty**, but this is of a different origin.

Kirstie: see **Kirsty**

Kirstin: see **Kirsten**

Kirsty Independently adopted Scottish diminutive of **Christine.** Spelling variant, **Kirstie,** also found, as for actress Kirstie Alley (born 1955).

Kit: see **Kitty**

Kittie: see **Kitty**

Kitty Independently adopted diminutive of **Katherine** or **Kathleen** (**Catherine**). Variant spelling is **Kittie,** while usual diminutive is **Kit.**

Kizzie: see **Keziah**

Kyle Australian name, probably adoption of male name **Kyle.** No regular variants or diminutives.

Kylie Australian name, probably development of **Kyle** or **Kelly.** Usual diminutive is **Kyle,** although this is really a different name.

Laetitia: see **Letitia**

Laila: see **Leila**

Lalage Greek name, from *lalagein*, "to prattle" or "to babble." Usual pronunciation is in three syllables (like "allergy") but with either hard or soft "g." Variant diminutives, **Lalla**, **Lallie**, and **Lally**, occur.

Lalla: see **Lalage**

Lallie: see **Lalage**

Lally: see **Lalage**

Lana Either from rare name **Alana**, itself feminine form of male **Alan**, or simply invention. No regular variants.

Lara Independently adopted diminutive of Russian name *Larissa*, itself linked with identically named ancient Greek city. No regular variants.

Laraine: see **Lorraine**

Laura Feminine form of Latin *laurus*, "laurel" or "bay," so figuratively "victory" or "triumph." Variants include **Lolly** and **Lori**, with others, **Lauren**, **Lauretta**, and **Laurie**, in independent use.

Lauren Probably independent variant of **Laura**, influenced by male name **Laurence**. Variants are mostly as for **Laura**.

Lauretta Independently adopted diminutive of **Laura**. Variant spelling, **Loretta**, has been adopted independently. Other variants are mainly diminutives as for **Laura**.

Laurie Independently adopted variant of **Laura**. Few regular variants.

Lavinia Feminine form of Latin place-name *Lavinium*, ancient town south of Rome. Main diminutive variants are **Vinnie** and **Vinny**.

Lea: see **Leah**

Leah Biblical name, from Hebrew *Le'ah*, "gazelle" or "antelope." Most common variant, **Lee**, is now an independent name. **Lea** also sometimes found.

Leda Greek name, itself perhaps representing a Lycian word meaning simply "woman." No variants recorded.

Lee Either feminine adoption of male name **Lee**, or diminutive of **Leah**, in independent use. **Leigh** is variant spelling.

Leigh: see **Lee**

Leila Arabic name, meaning "night," so of person "dark-haired," "dark-skinned," or "dark-eyed," implying oriental dusky beauty. Alternate spelling is **Laila**.

Lena Independently adopted diminutive of name such as **Helena**. Diminutive variant in independent use is **Leni**.

Leni Independently adopted diminutive of **Lena**. Few established variants.

Leona: see **Leonie**

Leonie From French feminine form (properly *Léonie*) of *Léon* (**Leon**). Variant, **Leona**, popular in the U.S.

Leonora Short form of **Eleonora**, itself a variant of **Eleanor**. Prime variant, diminutive **Nora**, is now an independent name.

Leontine French form (properly *Léontine*) of Italian *Leontina*, itself feminine form of Latin name *Leontius*, in turn derivative of **Leo**. Sometimes regarded as variant of **Leonora**, influenced by name such as **Clementine**. Alternate spelling, **Leontyne**, exists, as for opera singer Leontyne Price (born 1927) (original first names Mary Leontine).

Leontyne: see **Leontine**

Lesbia Greek name, meaning "woman of Lesbos" (largest of Greek islands). No regular variants.

Lesley Either from (Scottish) surname, which also gave male name **Leslie**, or directly as feminine form of latter. Main variant is **Leslie**, which is preferred in the U.S.

Leslie: see **Lesley**

Letitia From Latin *laetitia*, "joy" or "gladness." Variants include **Laetitia** and independently adopted **Lettice**. Diminutives include **Letty**, also now in use in own right, as well as **Tish**, **Tisha**, and **Titia**.

Lettice English vernacular form of **Letitia**. Most common variant is independently adopted diminutive, **Letty**.

Lettie: see **Letty**

Letty Independently adopted diminutive of **Lettice**, itself variant of **Letitia**. Most common variant is **Lettie**.

Letty: see **Alethea**

Lexy: see **Alexandra**

Lib: see **Libby**

Libby Independently adopted diminutive of **Elizabeth**, based on child's attempt to say this name. Main variant is further diminutive, **Lib.**

Lil: see **Lilian, Lillian,** and **Lily**

Lilian Probably independently adopted variant of **Elizabeth,** influenced by Italian *Liliana* and subsequently by **Lily.** Variant spelling, **Lillian,** exists in own right. Main diminutive is **Lil.**

Lillian Variant spelling of **Lilian,** established independently. Main diminutive is **Lil.**

Lily From name of flower, but also sometimes felt to be diminutive of **Elizabeth.** Variants include **Lil, Lillie,** and **Lilly.** Jersey-born actress Lillie Langtry (1853–1929), nicknamed "the Jersey Lily" for her beauty, had original first names Emilie Charlotte.

Lina Independent adoption of diminutive from some names ending *-lina,* such as **Adelina, Angelina,** Carolina (form of **Caroline**), and **Selina.** No established variants.

Linda Probably shortening of name such as **Belinda,** although Spanish *linda* means "pretty," and Italian *linda* means "neat" or "tidy." Variant spelling, **Lynda,** is in independent use, as is diminutive, **Lynn.** Another variant is **Lindy,** combining to form compounds such as **Lindybeth** and **Lindylou.**

Lindsay Feminine adoption of male name **Lindsay.** Variant spellings include **Lindsey, Lyndsey,** and **Lynsey.**

Lindsey: see **Lindsay**

Lindy: see **Linda**

Lindybeth: see **Linda**

Lindylou: see **Linda**

Linnet: see **Lynette**

Linnette: see **Lynette**

Lisa Independently adopted diminutive of **Elizabeth**, using European or "continental" spelling. Variant (and more common) spelling, **Liza**, is name in own right. Diminutives **Lisette** and **Lysette** exist.

Lisbeth Shortened form of **Elizabeth** used independently. Alternate spelling, **Lizbeth**, also found.

Lise: see **Elizabeth**

Lisette: see **Elizabeth** and **Lisa**

Livia Either shortened form of **Olivia** or feminine form of Roman clan name *Livius*, itself perhaps related to *lividus*, "leaden-colored." No regular variants.

Liz Independently adopted diminutive of **Elizabeth** or **Liza**. Main variant is **Lizzie**, in independent use.

Liza Diminutive of **Elizabeth** in independent use. Usual diminutives are **Liz** and **Lizzie**, with the latter in use in own right.

Lizbeth: see **Lisbeth**

Lizzie Independently adopted diminutive of **Elizabeth** or **Liza**. **Liz** is a directly related diminutive.

Lo: see **Lois**, **Lola**, **Lolita**, and **Loretta**

Lois Biblical name, explained as from Greek *lōiōn*, "more desirable" or "better," but now popularly associated with

Louisa and **Louise**. No regular variants, although **Lo** is occasionally found.

Lola Independently adopted diminutive of **Dolores**. Main variant is diminutive, **Lo**.

Lolita Independently adopted diminutive of **Dolores**. Common diminutives are **Lo** and **Lola**, with the latter now used independently.

Lolly: see **Laura**

Loraine: see **Lorraine**

Loretta Respelling of **Lauretta**, itself a diminutive of **Laura**. No regular variants, although diminutive, **Lo**, always possible.

Lori: see **Laura**

Lorna Invented by English novelist R.D. Blackmore for central character of novel *Lorna Doone* (1869). Blackmore claims he based name on Scottish place name Lorn, but he may also have had word "forlorn" in mind, because his tale begins with a child, Lorna, being kidnapped by Doones. No regular variants.

Lorraine From Scottish surname, but now felt to be variant of **Laura**. Variant spellings are **Laraine** and **Loraine**.

Lotta Independently adopted diminutive of **Charlotte**. **Lottie** is most common variant.

Lottie: see **Charlotte** and **Lotta**

Lotty: see **Charlotte**

Lou: see **Louella**, **Louisa**, and **Louise**

Louella Blend of **Lou** (diminutive of **Louisa**) and **Ella**. Few regular variants, but **Lou** is obvious candidate.

Louie: see **Louisa** and **Louise**

Louisa Feminine form of **Louis**. Main variants are diminutives, **Lou** and **Louie**.

Louise French form of **Louisa**. Main variants are diminutives, **Lou** and **Louie**, with **Lulu** now often in independent use.

Lu: see **Lucretia** and **Lulu**

Lucetta Independently adopted diminutive of **Lucia** or **Lucy**. Alternate spelling, **Lucette**, also occasionally found.

Lucette: see **Lucetta**

Lucia Feminine form of Roman clan name **Lucius**. Variants are mostly as for **Lucy**.

Lucile: see **Lucille**

Lucilla Latin diminutive of **Lucia**. Variants and diminutives are mostly as for **Lucy**, with **Lucille** now more common spelling.

Lucille French form of Latin name **Lucilla**. Variant spelling is **Lucile**, as for character Lucile McKelvey in Sinclair Lewis novel *Babbitt* (1923).

Lucinda Independently adopted variant of **Lucia** or **Lucy**. Variants mostly as for **Lucy**, as well as **Cindy**, now name in own right.

Lucky: see **Felicity** and **Lucy**

Lucretia Feminine form of Roman clan name *Lucretius*,

itself of uncertain origin (possibly related to **Lucius**). Few regular variants, though diminutive, **Lu**, always possible.

Lucy English form of Latin name **Lucia**. Main diminutive variant is **Lulu**, now sometimes found in independent use. **Lucky** also occasionally occurs.

Lulu Either independently adopted diminutive of **Louise** or **Lucy**, or from colloquial term "lulu" (itself probably from **Louise**). Further diminutive, **Lu**, also exists.

Lydia Biblical name of Greek origin meaning "woman of Lydia" (region of Asia Minor). No regular variants.

Lyn: see **Lynn**

Lynda Independently adopted spelling variant of **Linda**. Diminutive variant, **Lynn**, is in independent use.

Lyndsey: see **Lindsay**

Lynette Independently adopted diminutive of **Lynn**, formed by adding French feminine diminutive -*ette*. Variant spellings, **Linnet** and **Linnette**, came to be associated with linnet (songbird).

Lynn Diminutive form of **Linda** or **Lynda** used in own right, but also suggesting association with names ending -*line*, such as **Caroline** (which has modern variant spelling, **Carolyn**). Frequently spelled **Lynne**. **Lyn** also occurs.

Lynne: see **Lynn**

Lynsey: see **Lindsay**

Lysette: see **Lisa**

Mab: see **Mabel**

Mabel Shortened variant of **Amabel**, adopted in own right, but also interpreted as form of French *ma belle*, "my lovely." Usual variants are diminutives, **Mab** and **Mabs**.

Mabs: see **Mabel**

Maddy Independently adopted diminutive of **Madeleine** or **Madonna**. No regular variants.

Madeleine French form of **Magdalene**, sometimes popularly associated with "maid." English form of name, **Madeline**, has become adopted in own right, as has regular diminutive, **Maddy**.

Madeline English form of **Madeleine**. Diminutive variant, **Maddy**, is in independent use.

Madge Independently adopted diminutive of **Margaret**. No regular variants.

Madonna From (Italian) title of Virgin Mary (literally, "my lady"). Regular diminutives are **Donna** and **Maddy**, both in independent use.

Mae Variant of **May** in independent use. No regular variants.

Maev: see **Maeve**

Maeve English form of Irish *Meadhbh*, said to derive from Irish *meadhbhán*, "intoxication": meaning "she who inebriates." (Compare to related English *mead.*) Variant spelling is **Maev.**

Mag: see **Maggie**

Magda: see **Magdalene**

Magdala: see **Magdalene**

Magdalen: see **Magdalene**

Magdalene From biblical name of Mary Magdalene, "Mary of Magdala," related to **Madeleine.** Now felt to be more German than English, and associated by Germans with word *Magd,* "maid." Spelling variant is **Magdalen,** with main diminutives, **Magdala** and **Magda,** in use. Former of these is found for Magdala ("Maggie") Buckley in Agatha Christie novel *Peril at End House* (1932).

Maggie Independently adopted diminutive of **Margaret.** Further diminutives, **Mag** and **Mags,** sometimes occur.

Mags: see **Maggie**

Mahalia Perhaps adaptation of biblical name *Mahalath* (Genesis 28:9, 2 Chronicles 11:18), former wife of Esau, latter wife of king Rehoboam, this name in turn said to be a Hebrew musical term. Few regular variants.

Mai: see **May**

Maidie Probably direct from word "maid," but influenced by **Maisie.** Few regular variants, except alternate spelling, **Maidy.**

Maidy: see **Maidie**

Maisie Independently adopted variant of Scottish name *Mairead,* itself Gaelic form of **Margaret.** No regular variants.

Malandra Classical-style name that appears to be a blend of names such as **Melanie** and **Alexandra**. Too select to have established variants.

Malinda: see **Melinda**

Mally: see **Malvolia**

Malvina Apparently invented name, derived by eighteenth-century Scottish poet James Macpherson from Gaelic *mala mhìn*, "smooth brow." Few established variants.

Malvolia Presumably feminine equivalent of Shakespeare's *Malvolio* (meaning "ill-will"). Diminutive, **Mally**, recorded.

Mame: see **Mamie**

Mamie Independently adopted diminutive of **Margaret, Mary**, or (in extended form) **May**. Variant, **Mame**, popularized by musical and title-song of same name (1966).

Mandi: see **Mandy**

Mandy Independently adopted diminutive of **Amanda**. Variant spelling, **Mandi**, sometimes found.

Manon: see **Marie**

Mara Biblical name, traditionally said to mean "bitter," and popularly regarded as variant of **Mary**. Few established variants.

Marcia Feminine form of Latin name *Marcius*, related to **Marcus** and **Mark**. Now largely superseded by phonetically spelled variant, **Marsha**.

Margaret From Latin name *Margarita*, itself from Greek *margaron*, "pearl." Many diminutive variants include: independently adopted **Madge, Maggie, May, Meg**, and **Peggy**, and the more colloquial, **Marge** and **Margie**. Related also are **Marjory**, Welsh **Megan**, and various continental European equivalents, such as **Margarete** and **Margarita** (giving independent **Rita**), French **Margot** and **Marguerite**, also in independent use, and English equivalent, **Margo**, in independent use as well.

Margarete: see **Margaret**

Margarita: see **Margaret**

Margaux: see **Margot**

Marge: see **Margaret** and **Marjorie**

Margery: see **Marjorie**

Margie: see **Margaret** and **Marguerite**

Margo Independently adopted spelling of French **Margot**. No regular variants.

Margot French diminutive form of **Marguerite**, but as English name, regarded as diminutive of equivalent, **Margaret**. Main variant is independent spelling, **Margo**, but **Margaux** was adopted by actress Margaux Hemingway (born 1955), granddaughter of Ernest Hemingway, from French village *Margaux*.

Marguerite English adoption of French equivalent of **Margaret**, now also associated with garden flower. Compare to **Daisy**. **Margot** is a diminutive in regular use; others are **Margie** and **Margy**.

Margy: see **Marguerite**

Mari: see **Marie**

Maria Latin, modern Spanish, and Italian form of **Mary**.

French **Marie** and its diminutives are directly related, as is Italian diminutive, **Marietta**, in independent use.

Marian English form of French **Marion**, itself a diminutive of **Marie**, but more recently seen by some as blend of **Mary** and **Ann**. Independent variant spellings are **Mariana** and **Marianne**.

Mariana Latinized form of **Marian**, doubtlessly felt by some to be blend of **Maria** and **Anna**. Variant, **Marianna**, is in independent use.

Marianna Latinized form of **Marian** or **Marianne**, with the later felt to be blend of **Maria** and **Anna**. Directly related to variant, **Mariana**, also in independent use.

Marianne Independently adopted variant of **Marian**, with spelling as if to suggest blend of **Marie** (or **Mary**) and *Anne* (French form of **Ann**). Closely related variants are **Mariana** and **Marianna**, both in independent use.

Marie French form of **Mary**. French diminutive, **Manon**, exists, as for Massenet opera *Manon* (1884), based on Prévost novel *Manon Lescaut* (1731). Spelling variant, **Mari**, also exists, as for writers Mari Sandoz (1896–1966) and Mari Evans (born 1923).

Mariel Either short form of Italian *Mariella*, diminutive of **Maria**, or altered spelling of **Meriel** or **Muriel**. **Marielle** sometimes also occurs.

Marielle: see **Mariel**

Marietta English adoption of Italian diminutive of **Maria**. **Mariette**, French form of name, also found, as for actress Mariette Hartley (born 1940).

Mariette: see **Marietta**

Marigold From the flower. Diminutive, **Goldie**, is in independent use (but usually of a different origin).

Marilyn Blend of **Mary** and ending -*line* as in **Caroline**, but later felt to be compound of **Mary** and **Lynn**. Few regular variants.

Marina Feminine form of Roman clan name *Marinus*, itself diminutive of **Marius** but earlier associated with Latin *mare*, "sea," and in modern times with variants of **Mary**. No regular variants.

Marion French diminutive form of **Marie**. No regular variants.

Marje: see **Marjorie**

Marjorie Independent adoption of English vernacular form of **Margaret**. Popular variant is **Marjory**, while earlier spelling was usually **Margery**, familiar from nursery rhyme "See saw, Margery Daw." Common diminutives are **Marge** and **Marje**, with the former as for writer Marge Piercy (born 1936).

Marjory: see **Marjorie**

Marla: see **Marlene**

Marlene Contracted form of German *Maria Magdalene* (English, **Mary Magdalene**, in the Bible). Subsequently associated with **Marilyn**. Diminutive, **Marla**, sometimes found.

Marsha: see **Marcia**

Martha Biblical name, from Aramaic *Mārthā*, "lady." Most common variants are diminutives, **Marti**, **Martie**, and **Marty**. Independently adopted diminutive, **Mattie**, sometimes also evolves.

Marti: see **Martha** and **Martina**

Martie: see **Martha**

Martina Feminine form of **Martin.** Spelling variant is **Martine,** and usual diminutives are **Marti** and **Marty.**

Martine: see **Martina**

Marty: see **Martha** and **Martina**

Mary Beth: see **Beth**

Mary Jane: see **Jane**

Mary English form of French **Marie,** from Latin **Maria,** itself from Greek *Mariam,* in turn a form of Hebrew *Miryām,* which also gave biblical **Miriam.** Origin is uncertain, but name may represent root element *-mrh-* meaning "be fat," in a sense of "strong" or "excellent." Many variants and diminutives exist, several of which have been independently adopted, including **Mamie, May, Molly,** and **Polly.**

Matilda From Old German name *Mahthilda,* comprising *macht,* "might," and *hiltja,* "battle": "mighty in battle." Variant diminutives include independently adopted **Mattie** and **Tilly. Tilda** also exists. **Maud** is a directly related name.

Mattie Independently adopted diminutive of **Matilda.** Main variant is **Matty.**

Matty: see **Mattie**

Maud French contracted form of **Matilda.** Most common variant is diminutive, **Maudie.**

Maudie: see **Maud**

Maureen English form of Irish name *Máirín,* diminutive of

Máire (**Mary**). Rare spelling variants **Maurene, Maurine,** and **Moreen** exist.

Maurene: see **Maureen**

Maurine: see **Maureen**

Mave: see **Mavis**

Mavis From poetic word for song thrush. Diminutive variant, **Mave,** sometimes found.

Maxene: see **Maxine**

Maxie: see **Maxine**

Maxine Feminine form of **Max,** with *-ine* suffix from name such as **Caroline.** Alternate spelling, **Maxene,** exists, as for Maxene Andrews (born 1918), second of harmony trio The Andrews Sisters. Diminutive, **Maxie,** also found.

May Originally diminutive form of **Margaret** or **Mary,** subsequently regarded as flower or month name. Variants include **Mae,** in independent use, and **Mai.**

Maya Latin-style form of **May,** influenced by name of Roman goddess *Maia.* Few regular variants.

Meg Diminutive form of **Margaret** adopted independently. Most common variants are further diminutives, **Meggie** and **Megs.**

Megan Welsh form of **Meg,** itself a diminutive of **Margaret.** No regular variants exist, although **Meg** itself is possible, especially for non-Welsh bearer.

Meggie: see **Meg**

Megs: see **Meg**

Mel: see **Melanie** and **Melba**

Melanie French form of Latin name *Melania*, itself from Greek *melas*, "black," in sense of having dark hair, eyes, or skin. Diminutive, **Mel**, exists.

Melba From Australian operatic singer Nellie Melba (1861–1931) (original name Helen Mitchell), who adopted stage name from native city, Melbourne. Diminutive, **Mel**, likely to evolve.

Melina Probably shortening of name such as **Emmelina**, influenced by other *Mel-* names like **Melinda** or **Melissa.** No regular variants.

Melinda Probably formed on **Belinda**, with or without conscious reference to Latin *mel*, "honey." Spelling variant is **Malinda**.

Melissa From Greek *melissa*, "bee," itself from *meli*, "honey." Compare to **Deborah.** Diminutive variant, **Missie**, sometimes evolves.

Melody From the standard word, doubtless partly prompted by equation expressed in Irving Berlin song "A Pretty Girl is Like a Melody" (1919), partly by association with names such as **Melanie** and **Melissa.** Few regular variants.

Mercedes From Spanish *merced*, "mercy," with particular reference to title of Virgin Mary, *Maria de las Mercedes*, "Mary of the Mercies." Diminutive variants include **Mercy** and **Sadie**, both in independent use (although former normally has a different origin).

Mercy From the virtue. Former diminutive variant was **Merry**, now in independent use.

Meredith Adoption for female use of male name (see **Meredith**), but subsequently associated with **Merry**. Few regular variants.

Meriel Independently adopted variant of **Muriel**. Few regular variants exist, although **Merry** is possible. See also **Mariel**.

Merle Originally independently adopted variant of names such as **Meryl** and **Muriel**, but later associated with French *merle*, "blackbird." Compare to male name **Merle**. No regular variants.

Merry Either independently adopted diminutive of **Mercy**, or from standard word. No regular variants.

Meryl Independently adopted variant of **Muriel**. No regular variants exist, although **Merry** (in independent use), is logical development.

Mia From Scandinavian diminutive of **Maria**, independently adopted, although also "translated" as "my," from Spanish or Italian *mia*, with Italian *cara mia* ("my dear") a term of endearment. No regular variants.

Michaela Feminine form of **Michael**, usually pronounced "Mi*kay*la." No regular variants. Rare female use of male equivalent occurs for actress Michael Learned (born 1939).

Michèle French feminine form of *Michel* (**Michael**). This spelling is now often replaced by variant spelling, **Michelle**, and usually written without the accent, as for actress Michele Lee (born 1942).

Michelle Variant spelling of **Michèle**. No regular variants.

Midge Probably alteration of **Madge** or diminutive of name such as **Michelle**. Perhaps felt to be feminine equivalent of **Mick**. No established variants.

Mignon From French word (but not name) meaning, "cute" or "darling," also associated with flower *mignonette*. Diminutive, **Mignonette**, occasionally found.

Mignonette: see **Mignon**

Mildred From Old English name *Mildthrӯth*, comprising *milde*, "mild," and *thryth*, "strength": "gentle strength." Usual variants are independent diminutives **Millie** and **Milly**.

Millicent English variant of French *Mélisande*, itself from Old German name *Amalswint*, comprising *amal*, "industry" or "hard work," and *swind*, "strong": "hard worker." Common variants are diminutives **Millie** and **Milly**, also found independently.

Millie Independently adopted diminutive of **Camilla**, **Millicent**, and **Mildred**. Spelling variant, **Milly**, is probably more frequent and popular.

Milly Independently adopted diminutive of **Camilla**, **Millicent**, and **Mildred**. Most common variant is alternate spelling, **Millie**.

Mima: see **Jemima**

Mina Independently adopted diminutive of name such as **Wilhelmina**. Alternate spelling variant, **Minna**, is now in independent use.

Minerva From name of Roman goddess of wisdom, itself usually linked to Latin root *men-*, "mind." Usual variant is diminutive, **Minnie**, also found for other names.

Minna Independently adopted diminutive of name such as **Wilhelmina**. Alternate spelling, **Mina**, is in independent use.

Minnie Diminutive of **Wilhelmina** in independent use. Directly related to **Mina** and **Minna**, also in independent use.

Minta: see **Araminta**

Mira: see **Myra**

Mirabel From Latin *mirabilis*, "wonderful," but associated with French *belle*, "beautiful." No regular variants.

Miranda Devised by Shakespeare for main character (Prospero's daughter) in play *The Tempest* (1611), with meaning "fit to be admired" (compare to **Amanda**), from Latin *mirari*, "to wonder at." Variants are mainly diminutives, especially **Mandy** and **Randy**, both in independent use.

Miriam Biblical name, from Hebrew *Miryām*, which also gave **Mary**, and perhaps meaning "fat," or in a sense, "strong" or "fine." No regular variants.

Missie: see **Melissa**

Misty From standard word, evoking hazy island, autumn morning, and other similar images. No regular variants.

Mitzi German diminutive of **Maria**. No regular variants.

Modesty From ordinary word, regarded as "virtue." No regular variants.

Moira English form of Irish name *Máire* (**Mary**), with spelling to reflect pronunciation of latter. Alternate spelling variant is **Moyra**.

Moll: see **Molly**

Mollie: see **Molly**

Molly Independently adopted diminutive of **Mary**. Variant diminutive, **Moll**, is familiar from central character of Defoe novel *Moll Flanders* (1722). Alternate spelling, **Mollie**, also occurs.

Mona English form of Irish name *Muadhnait*, diminutive of *muadh*, "noble." No regular variants.

Monica Of uncertain origin. Has been associated with Greek *monos*, "alone," and Latin *monere*, "to warn" or "to advise." Diminutive variant, **Monny**, sometimes encountered.

Monny: see **Monica**

Morag English form of Scottish name *Mórag*, diminutive form of *Mór*, "great." No regular variants.

Moreen: see **Maureen**

Morgan Welsh name, perhaps from *mawr*, "great," and *can*, "bright," or with second element from *cant*, "circle." Compare to male name **Morgan**. Variant, **Morgana**, exists.

Morgana: see **Morgan**

Moyra: see **Moira**

Muriel Probably English variant of Irish name *Muirgheal*, comprising *muir*, "sea," and *geal*, "bright": "sea-bright." **Meriel** is independently adopted variant, as **Mariel** also can be.

Myf: see **Myfanwy**

Myfanwy Welsh name, comprising prefix *my-* denoting affection, *manwy*, "fine" or "rare": "dear fine one." Name is pronounced approximately "Mu*van*wy." Diminutive variant, **Myf** (pronounced "Muv"), sometimes found.

Myra Invented by seventeenth-century English poet Fulke Greville, perhaps based on Greek *myron*, "myrrh," or Latin *mirari*, "to wonder at" (compare to **Miranda**), or even as anagram of **Mary**. Later associated with **Moira**. Variant spelling, **Mira**, occasionally found.

Myrna English form of Irish name *Muirne*, from *muirne*, "tenderness" or "affection." Few regular variants.

Myrtle From the plant, with its pink or white flowers and aromatic berries. No regular variants.

Nadia Diminutive of Russian name *Nadezhda* (**Hope**). Spelling variant, **Nadya** (representing more precisely a Russian diminutive), sometimes found.

Nadine French elaboration of **Nadia**. No regular variants.

Nadya: see **Nadia**

Nan Independent adoption of diminutive of **Ann**, and subsequently also of **Nancy**. No regular variants, although **Nana** is a directly related name.

Nana Independently adopted diminutive of **Ann**, later felt to be a variant of **Nan**. Few regular variants.

Nance: see **Nancy**

Nanci: see **Nancy**

Nancy Independently adopted diminutive of **Ann** or some similar but now abandoned medieval name. Compare to **Nan**. Variant spelling, **Nanci**, sometimes occurs, as for country singer Nanci Griffith (born 1953). Main diminutive is **Nance**, as for Nance Mockridge in Hardy novel *The Mayor of Casterbridge* (1886).

Nanette Independently adopted diminutive of **Nan**. Sometimes has spelling variant, **Nannette**.

Nannette: see **Nanette**

Naomi Biblical name, from Hebrew *Nā'omī*, "my delight." No established variants. See also **Mara**.

Natalia: see **Natalie**

Natalie French form of Russian *Natalya*, itself from Latin *dies natalis*, "birthday," specifically *dies natalis Domini*, "birthday of the Lord," i.e., "Christmas" (compare to **Noel**). Spelling variant **Natalia**, closer to original Russian, sometimes found, as promoted by Russian-born ballerina Natalia Makarova (born 1940).

Natasha Russian diminutive of *Natalya* (**Natalie**). Variant spellings include **Natashia** and **Natashya**, and a diminutive, **Tasha**, is sometimes found.

Natashia: see **Natasha**

Natashya: see **Natasha**

Nell Independently adopted diminutive of **Eleanor**, **Ellen**, and **Helen**. Diminutive variant, **Nellie**, is in independent use.

Nella: see **Fenella**

Nellie Independently adopted diminutive of **Nell**. Alternate spelling, **Nelly**, quite common.

Nelly: see **Nellie**

Nerissa Probably based on Greek *nērēis*, "nymph." No regular variants.

Nerys Welsh name, perhaps intended as feminine form of *nĕr*, "lord," but associated with **Nerissa** by English speakers. No regular variants.

Nessa: see **Vanessa**

Nessie Independently adopted diminutive of **Agnes** or **Vanessa**. No regular variants.

Nest: see **Nesta**

Nesta Welsh diminutive form of **Agnes**, adopted independently. Diminutive variant, **Nest**, was actually an original form of a Welsh name.

Netta Independent adoption either of **Nettie** or of names ending -*netta* or -*nette*, such as **Annette**. No regular variants.

Nettie Independently adopted diminutive of name ending -*nette* such as **Annette**. Main variant is alternate spelling, **Netty**, as for central character of Hardy short story "Netty Sargent's Copyhold" in *Life's Little Ironies* (1894).

Netty: see **Nettie**

Nib: see **Isabel**

Nichola: see **Nicola**

Nick: see **Nicola**

Nicki: see **Nicola**

Nickie: see **Nicola**

Nicola Feminine form of **Nicholas** (which in Italian is identically *Nicola*). Fairly common variant spellings include **Nichola** and French **Nicole**. Among many diminutives are **Nick, Nicki, Nickie, Nikki,** and **Nicolette**, with the last of these containing the French diminutive suffix -*ette*.

Nicole: see **Nicola**

Nicolette: see **Nicola**

Nikki: see **Nicola**

Nina Russian diminutive of *Antonina* (**Antonia**). No regular variants.

Nita: see **Anita** and **Juanita**

Noel From French *noël*, "Christmas," and frequently given to children born at this time. Popular variant spellings are **Noele** and **Noelle**, both sometimes with dieresis, and Noel itself can also be Noël.

Noele: see **Noel**

Noelle: see **Noel**

Nora Independently adopted diminutive of name such as **Eleonora** (form of **Eleanor**), Honora (form of **Honor**), and **Leonora**. Most common variant is alternate spelling, **Norah**.

Norah: see **Nora**

Norma Probably adoption of standard Latin (or Italian) word *norma*, "norm," "rule," or "standard." Now often regarded as feminine form of **Norman**. No regular variants.

Nyree English spelling of Maori name *Ngaire*, of uncertain meaning. No regular variants.

Octavia Feminine form of Latin name **Octavius**. No regular variants.

Odetta: see **Odette**

Odette Independently adopted feminine diminutive of Old French name *Oda*, itself related to **Otto**. Variant form is **Odetta**.

Olave: see **Olive**

Olga Russian name, feminine form of *Oleg* and equivalent of Scandinavian *Helga*, "holy." No regular variants.

Olive From the plant, which itself implies peace ("olive branch"). Occasional variant spelling, **Olave**, as for Girl Scout founder Lady Olave Baden-Powell (1889–1977), wife of Lord Robert Baden-Powell, founder of Boy Scouts. Diminutive, **Olivette**, also formerly in use.

Olivette: see **Olive**

Olivia From Latin or (later) Italian *oliva*, "olive." Now sometimes regarded as feminine equivalent of **Oliver**. No regular variants.

Olwen Welsh name, from *ôl*, "footprint" or "track," and *gwen*, "white" or "fair": "white footprints." No regular variants.

Ona Either alteration of **Oona** or adoption of final letters of name such as **Fiona**. No regular variants.

Oona English form of Irish name **Una**. Variant spelling, **Oonagh**, exists.

Oonagh: see **Oona**

Opal From the precious stone. No regular variants.

Ophelia Apparently feminine of Greek name *Ōphelos*, meaning "profit" or "help," perhaps in sense, "helpmate" or "wife." No regular variants.

Oprah Variant of biblical name *Orpah*, itself said to mean "she who turns her back." No regular variants, apart from original name.

Oriana Perhaps from Latin *oriri*, "to rise," so meaning "dawn" or "sunrise" (compare to **Dawn**), or else based on word that gave French *or*, "gold." No regular variants.

Orinthia Perhaps from Greek *orinein*, "to excite" or "to stir the mind." No recorded variants.

Ottoline Independently adopted diminutive of French (or German) *Ottilie*, itself from medieval name *Odila*, feminine form of **Otto**. No established variants.

Pam Independently adopted diminutive of **Pamela**. Few regular variants.

Pamela Invented by English poet Sir Philip Sidney for prose romance *The Arcadia* (1590), perhaps from Greek *pan*, "all," and *meli*, "honey": "all sweetness." He stressed name on second syllable, "Pamela." Main variant is diminutive, **Pam**, in use in own right. Alternate spelling, **Pamella**, occurs.

Pamella: see **Pamela**

Pandora Greek name, from *pan*, "all," and *dōron*, "gift": "many gifted." No regular variants although diminutive, **Dora** (now independent name), is possible.

Pansy From the flower, itself associated with thought, (French *pensée*). No regular variants.

Parthenia Greek name, from *parthenos*, "virgin." Few, if any, variants exist.

Parthenope Greek name, from *parthenos*, "virgin" (as for **Parthenia**), and *ōps*, "face": "maiden-faced." No regular variants.

Pat Independently adopted diminutive of **Patricia** (as male **Pat** is for **Patrick**). Usual diminutives are **Patti** and **Patty**, both in independent use.

Patience From the virtue. No regular variants or diminutives.

Patricia Feminine form of Latin *Patricius*, "noble man," but later regarded as female equivalent of **Patrick**. Diminutive variant, **Pat**, is most common and in independent use, as are the less common **Patsy**, **Patti**, and **Patty**. **Tricia**, **Trish**, and **Trisha** are all likewise found.

Patsy Independently adopted diminutive of **Patricia**. Few regular variants, although **Pat** is always possible.

Patti Independently adopted spelling of **Patty**. Variant spelling, **Pattie**, also found.

Pattie: see **Patti**

Patty Individually adopted diminutive of name such as **Martha**, **Matilda**, and (later) **Patricia**. Variant spelling, **Patti**, is in independent use.

Paula Feminine form of **Paul**. No regular variants.

Pauleen: see **Pauline**

Paulene: see **Pauline**

Paulette Independently adopted French feminine diminutive of **Paul**. No regular variants.

Paulina Feminine form of Latin name *Paulinus*, itself a diminutive of *Paulus* (**Paul**). No regular variants.

Pauline French form of **Paulina**. Occasional variant spellings, **Paulene** and **Pauleen**, are found.

Pearl From the gem. Sometimes diminutive, **Pearlie**, is found.

Pearlie: see **Pearl**

Peg: see **Peggy**

Peggy Independently adopted variant of **Maggie**, itself a diminutive of **Margaret.** Usual diminutive variant is **Peg.**

Pen: see **Penny**

Penelope Greek name, perhaps based on *pēnē*, "thread": "seamstress." Common variant is diminutive, **Penny,** in independent use.

Penny Independently adopted diminutive of **Penelope.** Occasional further diminutive, **Pen,** is sometimes found.

Perdita From Shakespeare character in *The Winter's Tale* (1610), deriving from Latin *perdita*, "lost." No regular variants.

Perry: see **Persephone** and **Persis**

Persephone Greek name, comprising *pherein*, "to bring," and *phonē*, "death": "bringing death." No regular variants or diminutives, although **Perry** is possible.

Persis Biblical name, from Greek meaning "Persian woman." No regular variants, although diminutive, **Perry,** is possible.

Pet: see **Petula**

Peta Feminine equivalent of **Peter.** No regular variants.

Petra Latinized feminine equivalent of **Peter.** Few regular variants.

Petronella English form of Latin name *Petronilla*, feminine diminutive of Roman clan name *Petronius*, long associated with **Peter.** Few regular variants.

Petula Perhaps from Latin *petere*, "to seek" or "to beg," as if "one sought for," or from Latin *petulans*, "bold." Now sometimes felt to be related to **Peter**, or to suggest "petal" or even "pet." Variant diminutive, **Pet**, is possible.

Phil: see **Philadelphia** and **Philomena**

Philadelphia Biblical name (of place, not person), from Greek name meaning "brotherly love," i.e. (in Christian terms), "one who loves the brethren." No regular variants, but diminutive, **Phil**, would be natural development.

Philippa Feminine equivalent of **Philip**. Most common variant is diminutive, **Pippa**, now an independent name.

Phillis: see **Phyllis**

Phillys: see **Phyllis**

Philomel: see **Philomela**

Philomela Greek name, comprising *philos*, "dear" or "sweet," and *melos*, "song": "sweet singer" or (from *philomela*, combining two elements), "nightingale." Alternate spelling, **Philomel**, also found.

Philomena Greek name, comprising *philein*, "to love," and *menos*, "strength": "strength-loving" or "strongly loved." No regular variants, although diminutive, **Phil**, possible, as for all names beginning *Phil-*.

Phoebe Biblical name, from Greek *phoibe*, "bright." No regular variants.

Phyllis Greek name, from *phyllis*, "foliage" or "green branch." Variant spellings are **Phillis** and **Phillys**.

Pia From Latin or Italian *pia* (feminine of *pius*, *pio* respectively), "pious" or "obedient" (to parents). No regular variants.

Piety From the virtue. No regular variants.

Pip: see **Pippa**

Pippa Independently adopted diminutive of **Philippa**. Variant diminutive, **Pip**, sometimes found.

Plaxy Cornish name, said to be form of Greek name *Praxedes*, "active," from *praxis*, "action" or "doing." Few regular variants.

Pleasance From archaic English word meaning "pleasure" or "happiness." No regular variants exist, although **Pleasant** is closely related.

Pleasant From ordinary word. No regular variants, although **Pleasance** is closely related.

Poll: see **Polly**

Polly Independently adopted variant of **Molly**, itself a diminutive of **Mary**. **Poll** is a common diminutive, and **Pollyanna** is a directly derived name.

Pollyanna Combination of **Polly** and **Anna**. No regular variants.

Poppy From the flower. No regular variants.

Portia From Latin name *Porcia*, feminine of Roman clan name *Porcius*, itself of uncertain origin but perhaps derived from *porcus*, "pig." No regular variants.

Posy Originally independent adoption of diminutive of **Josephine**, but now usually associated with standard word for bunch of flowers. No regular variants.

Primrose From the flower. No regular variants.

Priscilla Biblical name, feminine diminutive of Roman clan name *Priscus*, itself meaning "previous" or "ancient." Variant diminutives include **Cilla**, now an independent name, and **Prissy**, as for Prissy Jakin, character in George Eliot novel *The Mill on the Floss* (1860).

Prissy: see **Priscilla**

Proserpine From Roman name for **Persephone**, related by some to Latin *proserpere*, "to creep forth," as of flowers in spring. No regular variants, although diminutives **Pross** and **Prossy**, have been recorded.

Pross: see **Proserpine**

Prossy: see **Proserpine**

Pru: see **Prudence** and **Prunella**

Prudence From the virtue. Most common variants are diminutives **Pru** and **Prue**. Early literary example of latter is country girl Miss Prue in Congreve comedy *Love for Love* (1695).

Prue: see **Prudence** and **Prunella**

Prunella Plant name, botanically that of selfheal (*Prunella vulgaris*), influenced by late Latin *prunella*, "little plum." Variants are diminutives, **Pru** and **Prue**, as for **Prudence**.

Psyche Greek name, from *psychē*, "soul." No regular variants.

Queenie Independently adopted diminutive of nickname "Queen." Few regular variants.

Rachael: see **Rachel**

Racheal: see **Rachel**

Rachel Biblical name, from Hebrew *Rāhēl*, "ewe." Alternate spellings include **Rachael** (presumably influenced by **Michael**), **Racheal**, and Spanish form, **Raquel**, in independent use. Diminutives, **Rachie**, **Rae**, and **Ray**, also occur.

Rachie: see **Rachel**

Rae: see **Rachel**

Ramona Feminine form of Spanish *Ramón* (**Raymond**). Few regular variants.

Randy Either feminine use of male name **Randy** or as independently adopted diminutive of **Miranda**. No regular variants.

Raquel Spanish form of **Rachel** in independent use. No regular variants.

Ray: see **Rachel**

Rebecca Biblical name, from Hebrew *Ribhqāh*, perhaps form of *Biqrah*, "cow" (compare to **Leah**). Best-known variant is diminutive **Becky**, in independent use.

Regina From Latin *regina*, "queen." Diminutive variant, **Gina**, is an independent name. French form of name, **Régine**, also exists.

Régine: see **Regina**

Rene: see **Irene**

René: see **Renée**

Renée French feminine of **René**. Spelling variant, **René**, is also found. English pronunciation of name as "Renny" has led to variant spellings, **Rennie** and **Renny**, among others.

Rennie: see **Renée**

Renny: see **Renée**

Rhoda Biblical name, itself from Greek, either from *rhodon*, "rose," or meaning "woman of Rhodes." No regular variants.

Rhona Scottish name, perhaps from island of Rona, with spelling alteration influenced by **Rhoda**. Variant spelling, **Rona**, is in independent use.

Rhonda Apparently a blend of **Rhoda** and **Rhona**. Few regular variants.

Rica: see **Frederica**

Rickie: see **Frederica**

Ricky: see **Frederica**

Rita Independently adopted diminutive of Spanish *Margarita* or Italian *Margherita* (**Margaret**), or some similar name ending -*rita*. No regular variants.

Roberta Feminine form of **Robert**. Diminutive variant, **Berta**, occurs.

Robin Feminine adoption of male name **Robin**, perhaps influenced by name of bird. Variant spelling, **Robyn**, also found.

Robyn: see **Robin**

Rona Scottish name, either independently adopted variant of **Rhona**, or from Scottish island of Rona. Also regarded as feminine form of **Ronald**. Few variants.

Ronnie: see **Veronica**

Roo: see **Rue** and **Ruth**

Rosa Latin or Italian form of **Rose**. Name (or Latin *rosa* which gave it), lies behind many independently adopted derivatives, such as **Rosalba, Rosalie, Rosalind, Rosaline, Rosamund, Rosanna, Rosemary, Rosina,** and **Rosita**.

Rosalba Apparently compound of Latin *rosa*, "rose," and *alba*, "white": "white rose." Variant diminutives are as for **Rose**.

Rosalie French form of Latin or Italian name *Rosalia*, itself based on *rosa*, "rose" (compare to **Rosa** and **Rose**). Variant diminutives are mainly as for **Rose**.

Rosalind Probably from Late Latin *rosa linda*, "pretty rose," although derived by some from Old German *hros*, "steed" or "horse," and *linta*, "lime" or "shield made of lime wood": "horse shield." Variant, **Rosaline**, is independent name, while diminutives are as for **Rose**.

Rosaline Independently adopted variant of **Rosalind**. Variant spelling, **Rosalyn**, exists. Diminutives are mostly as for **Rose**.

Rosalyn: see **Rosaline**

Rosamond: see **Rosamund**

Rosamund Probably from Late Latin *rosa munda*, "pure rose," or *rosa mundi*, "rose of the world," but traced back by some to Old German *hros*, "steed" or "horse," and *munt*, "protection": "horse protection." Variant spelling, **Rosamond**, is common.

Rosanna Compound of **Rose** and **Anna**, perhaps suggested by **Roxana**. Variant spellings include **Rosannah, Rosanne**, and **Roseanne**, with the latter two respectively as for singer Rosanne Cash (born 1955) and actress Roseanne Barr (born 1952).

Rosannah: see **Rosanna**

Rosanne: see **Rosanna**

Rose Long connected with flower name, but traced back by some to Old German *hros*, "steed" or "horse," or *hrōd*, "fame." Main variant is **Rosa**, formerly standard written form of name. Diminutives are **Rosie**, now an independent name, **Rosey** and **Rosy**.

Roseanne: see **Rosanna**

Rosemarie: see **Rosemary**

Rosemary From plant name, but also taken as compound of **Rose** and **Mary**. Most common variant is **Rosemarie** (sometimes as two words), popularized by romantic musical *Rose Marie* (1924) and its title song.

Rosetta Independently adopted Italian diminutive of *Rosa* (**Rose**). French variant, **Rosette**, is still occasionally found.

Rosette: see **Rosetta**

Rosey: see **Rose** and **Rosie**

Rosie Independently adopted diminutive of **Rose**. (Compare to **Rosa** and **Rosemary**.) Alternate spellings **Rosey** and **Rosy** exist.

Rosina Italian-style diminutive of **Rosa** (**Rose**). Diminutive variants are mainly as for **Rose**.

Rosita English adoption of Spanish diminutive of **Rosa** (**Rose**). Diminutives are mainly as for **Rose**.

Rosy: see **Rose** and **Rosie**

Rowena Either form of Welsh name *Rhonwen*, said to comprise *rhon*, "pike" or "lance," and *gwen*, "white" or "fair": "slender and fair," or modern version of (unrecorded) Old German name comprising *hrōd*, "fame," and *wynn*, "joy." Few regular variants.

Roxana From Persian name *Roschana* (**Dawn**). Variant spellings, **Roxane** and **Roxanne**, exist, as do diminutives, **Roxie** and **Roxy**.

Roxane: see **Roxana**

Roxanne: see **Roxana**

Roxie: see **Roxana**

Roxy: see **Roxana**

Rubie: see **Ruby**

Ruby From the gem. Variant form, **Rubie**, occasionally found.

Rue From the plant, although also regarded as diminutive of **Ruth**. No regular variants, although spelling, **Roo**, occasionally occurs.

Roo: see **Rue**

Ruth Biblical name, perhaps from Hebrew *rēkuth*, "friend" or "companion," but (at first) associated with English word "ruth," meaning "compassion" (source of modern "ruthless"). Diminutive variants, **Roo** and **Ruthie**, exist.

Ruthie: see **Ruth**

Sabbie: see **Sabina** and **Sabrina**

Sabby: see **Sabina** and **Sabrina**

Sabina From Latin name *Sabina*, "Sabine woman." Sometimes associated with **Sabrina**, but that is a different name. Diminutives include **Sabbie**, **Sabby**, and **Bina**.

Sabrina From name of maiden in Celtic legend said to have given name of the Severn River. Diminutives, **Sabbie** and **Sabby**, exist. Name is not related to **Sabina**, which has a different origin.

Sacha: see **Sasha**

Sadie Independently adopted diminutive of **Sarah**. No regular variants.

Sal: see **Sally**

Sally Independently adopted diminutive of **Sarah**. Name often coupled with others to form compounds, especially **Sally Ann** and **Sally Jane** (often hyphenated). Usual diminutive is **Sal**.

Sally Ann: see **Sally**

Sally Jane: see **Sally**

Salome Biblical name, from Hebrew *shālōm*, "peace." No regular variants.

Sam: see **Samantha**

Samantha Probably feminine form of **Samuel**, perhaps influenced by name such as **Anthea**. Derived by some, however, from Greek *psamathos*, "sandy shore." Common variant diminutives, increasingly popular from 1970s, are **Sam** and **Sammy**.

Sammy: see **Samantha**

Sandie: see **Sandy**

Sandra Independently adopted diminutive of Italian *Alessandra* (**Alexandra**). Occasional variants **Saundra** and **Sondra** occur in the U.S., with the latter familiar from actress Sondra Locke (born 1947). Usual diminutive is **Sandy**, now an independent name.

Sandy Independently adopted diminutive of **Alexandra** or **Sandra**. Variant spelling, **Sandie**, is quite common.

Sara Independently adopted spelling variant of **Sarah**. No regular variants.

Sarah Jane: see **Jane**

Sarah Biblical name, from Hebrew *Sārāh*, "princess." Alternate spelling, **Sara**, is in independent use, as are diminutives, **Sadie** and **Sally**. **Sassie** can also be also found.

Sarah Jane: see **Jane**

Sasha English adoption of Russian diminutive of **Alexandra**. Compare to male name **Sasha**. French variant spelling, **Sacha**, sometimes found.

Sassie: see **Sarah**

Saundra: see **Sandra**

Scarlet: see **Scarlett**

Scarlett From surname, but also suggesting bright color "scarlet." Few regular variants, although **Scarlet** is on record.

Selena: see **Selina**

Selima Perhaps variant of Arabic name *Selim*, "peace" (compare to **Salome**). No regular variants.

Selina Form of Greek *Sēlēnē*, name of goddess of moon, from *sēlēnē*, "moon." Variant, **Selena**, sometimes found.

Serena Feminine form of Latin *serenus*, "calm" or "serene." No regular variants.

Shari: see **Sharon**

Sharmain: see **Charmaine**

Sharmaine: see **Charmaine**

Sharon Biblical name, but that of place (valley in Palestine), not person, itself from Hebrew *Sarōn*, probably from *sar*, "to sing" or "singer." Variant spelling, **Sharron**, is fairly common, and **Sharyn** is also found. Diminutive is **Shari**, as for Canadian ventriloquist (with "Lamb Chop"), Shari Lewis (born 1930). Variant, **Sharona,** was promoted by The Knack song "My Sharona" (1979).

Sharona: see **Sharon**

Sharron: see **Sharon**

Sharyn: see **Sharon**

Sheba Independently adopted diminutive of **Bathsheba**. No established variants.

Sheena English form of Scottish Síne (**Jane**). Variant spelling, **Sheenagh**, sometimes found, perhaps influenced by **Shelagh**.

Sheenagh: see **Sheena**

Sheila English form of Irish name *Síle* (**Celia**). Variant spelling, **Shelagh**, quite common, as for Irish playwright Shelagh Delaney (born 1939).

Shelagh: see **Sheila**

Shelley Adapted form of **Shirley**, influenced by surname Shelley (as for the English poet). Few regular variants.

Sheree: see **Cherie**

Sheri: see **Cherie**

Sherie: see **Cherie**

Sherill: see **Cheryl**

Sherilyn: see **Cheryl**

Sherley: see **Shirley**

Sherry Either Anglicized form of French **Cherie**, or independently adopted diminutive of **Shirley**, either way influenced by "sherry" (fortified wine). Few regular variants.

Sheryl: see **Cheryl**

Shirl: see **Shirley**

Shirlee: see **Shirley**

Shirley From surname. Several rare variant spellings exist, such as **Sherley** and **Shirlee**, with the most common diminutive being **Shirl**.

Siân Welsh form of **Jane**, pronounced "Shahn," often regarded as feminine equivalent of **Sean**. Also spelled without accent, and having diminutive variant, **Siani**.

Siani: see **Siân**

Sib: see **Isabel** and **Sybil**

Sibyl: see **Sybil**

Sidney Feminine adoption of male name **Sidney**, perhaps prompted by **Sidonie**. Alternate spelling, **Sydney**, exists, while rare **Sydne** is found for actress Sydne Rome (born 1946).

Sidonie French form of Latin name *Sidonia*, "woman of Sidon" (capital of ancient Phoenicia). Alternate spelling, **Sidony**, occurs, and this may have prompted female **Sidney**.

Sidony: see **Sidonie**

Silvia Feminine form of Latin name *Silvius*, itself derived from *silva*, "wood." Variant spelling, **Sylvia**, has now all but superseded original form.

Simmie: see **Simone**

Simmy: see **Simone**

Simona: see **Simone**

Simone French feminine form of, and equivalent of the English name, **Simon**. Variant form is **Simona**, and most common diminutives are **Simmie** and **Simmy**.

Sindy: see **Cindy**

Sinead Irish form (properly *Sinéad*) of **Janet**, pronounced "Shinade." No regular variants.

Siobhan Irish form (properly *Siobhán*) of **Joan**, pronounced "Shi*vawn*." No regular variants.

Sissy: see **Cissie**

Skeeter From nickname, usually for active or small person (from "mosquito" or for someone who "skeets," i.e., scoots). No regular variants.

Sofia: see **Sophia**

Sondra: see **Sandra**

Sonia Russian diminutive of *Sofiya* (**Sophia**). Variant spellings are **Sonya** and **Sonja**, with the former familiar from film writer Sonya Levien (1888–1960), and the latter from Norwegian-American ice skater Sonja Henje (1910–1969).

Sonja: see **Sonia**

Sonya: see **Sonia**

Sophia From Greek word meaning "wisdom." Variant, **Sophie**, is an independent name, as is diminutive, **Sonya**. Variant spelling, **Sofia**, also exists.

Sophie French form of **Sophia**, adopted independently. Alternate spelling, **Sophy**, also found, as for Sophy Gauntlet in Smollett novel *Peregrine Pickle* (1751).

Sophronia Greek name, from *sōphrōn*, "prudent" or "sensible." No regular variants. Diminutive, **Sophie**, is usually more related to **Sophia**.

Sophy: see **Sophie**

Spring From the season, considered the most attractive of year, and also suggesting a source of clear running water. No variants.

Stace: see **Stacy**

Stacey: see **Stacy**

Staci: see **Stacy**

Stacie: see **Stacy**

Stacy Either independently adopted diminutive of **Anastasia**, or, more likely, from feminine adoption of male name **Stacy**. Variant spellings include **Stacey, Staci,** and **Stacie.** Usual diminutive is **Stace.**

Stef: see **Stephanie**

Stefanie: see **Stephanie**

Steffie: see **Stephanie**

Stella From Latin *stella,* "star." Few regular variants, but **Estelle** is directly related.

Stephanie French form (properly *Stéphanie*) of Latin *Stephania,* or *Stephana,* feminine equivalent of *Stephanus* (**Stephen**). Variants include **Stefanie,** as for actress Stefanie Powers (born 1942) (original name Stefania Federkiewicz), **Stef, Steffie,** and **Stevie.**

Stevie: see **Stephanie**

Storm From standard word, perhaps implying passionate nature. No apparent variants.

Su: see **Sue**

Sue Independently adopted diminutive of **Susan,** or (less often) **Susannah.** Variant spelling, **Su,** is becoming increasingly common.

Sukie: see **Susan**

Suky: see **Susan**

Sunday From day of week. No regular diminutives exist but **Sunny** is a likely development.

Susan Shortened form of **Susannah**, adopted independently. Many diminutives include **Sue, Susie** (both in independent use), **Sukie**, and **Suky. Suzanne** relates more to **Susannah**.

Susanna: see **Susannah**

Susannah Biblical name, from Hebrew *shūshannāh*, "lily." Most common variant is **Susanna**, popularized in Stephen Foster song "Oh! Susanna" (1848). French variant, **Suzanne**, is in independent use, with diminutives as for **Susan**.

Susie Independently adopted diminutive of **Susan** or **Susannah**. Variant spellings **Suzi, Suzie**, and **Suzy** exist.

Suzanne French form of **Susannah**. Diminutives are as for **Susie**.

Suzi: see **Susie**

Suzie: see **Susie**

Suzy: see **Susie**

Sybil From Greek name *Sibylla* or *Sybilla*, generally given to various prophetesses, and itself of obscure origin. Variant spelling, **Sibyl**, also still sometimes found. Rare variant, **Cybill**, familiar from actress Cybill Shepherd (born 1949). Diminutive, **Sib**, also exists.

Sydne: see **Sidney**

Sydney: see **Sidney**

Syl: see **Sylvia**

Sylvette: see **Sylvia**

Sylvia Independently adopted variant spelling of **Silvia**. French variant, **Sylvie**, sometimes found. Usual diminutive is **Syl**, but French-style **Sylvette** is also found.

Sylvie: see **Sylvia**

Tabby: see **Tabitha**

Tabitha Biblical name, from Aramaic *Tabhītha*, "gazelle."
Former stock diminutive was **Tabby**. See also **Dorcas**.

Tamar Biblical name, from Hebrew *Tāmar*, "date palm."
Former diminutive was **Tammy**, now an independent name.

Tamara Russian adoption of **Tamar**, with final feminine *-a*.
Diminutive, **Tammy**, is name in own right.

Tammie: see **Tammy**

Tammy Independently adopted diminutive of **Tamara**,
Tamsin, and **Tansy**. Spelling variant, **Tammie**, occurs.

Tamsin Contracted form of **Thomasin**, adopted for
independent use. Usual diminutive is **Tammy**, now an
independent name.

Tania: see **Tanya**

Tansy From name of flower. No regular variants, although
diminutive, **Tammy**, is on record.

Tanya Russian diminutive of **Tatiana**, adopted independently.
Spelling variant, **Tania**, is also found.

Tasha: see **Natasha**

Tatiana Russian name, itself originally from Roman clan
name *Tatius*. Variant diminutive, **Tanya**, is in independent
use.

Teena: see **Tina**

Teresa Variant of **Theresa**, adopting Spanish or Italian form. Diminutives, **Terry**, **Tess**, **Tessa**, and **Tracy**, are all in independent use.

Teri: see **Terry**

Terri: see **Terry**

Terry Either independently adopted diminutive of **Theresa** or adoption of male name **Terry**. Variant spellings, **Terri** and **Teri**, exist, with the latter as for actress Teri Garr (born 1952).

Tess Independently adopted diminutive of **Theresa** or **Tessa**. Diminutives are as for **Tessa**.

Tessa Independently adopted diminutive of **Theresa**, although regarded by some as of a different, possibly continental European origin. Diminutive, **Tess**, is in independent use. **Tessie** is also found.

Tessie: see **Tessa**

Thea Diminutive form of **Dorothea**, used in own right, and perhaps regarded by some as equivalent to male **Theo**. No regular variants.

Theda: see **Theodora**

Thelma Perhaps from Greek *thelēma*, "will" or "wish." No regular variants.

Theo: see **Theodora** and **Theodosia**

Theodora Feminine form of **Theodore**. Diminutives include independently adopted **Dora**, **Theda**, and **Theo**.

Theodosia Greek name, comprising *theos*, "god," and *dōsis*, "giving": "God's gift." Main diminutives are **Dosia** and **Theo**.

Theresa Origin uncertain. May have evolved either from Greek *therizein*, "to harvest," or from name of Aegean island of *Thera*. Main variant is **Teresa**, but French **Thérèse** is also sometimes found. Diminutives are now mostly in independent use, including **Terry**, **Tess**, and **Tessa**.

Thérèse: see **Theresa**

Thomasa: see **Thomasin**

Thomasin Feminine form of **Thomas**. Variants include **Thomasa**, **Thomasina**, and independent shortened form, **Tamsin**. Few regular diminutives.

Thomasina: see **Thomasin**

Tiff: see **Tiffany**

Tiffany English form of Greek name *Theophania*, "Epiphany," given to girls born on January 6. Diminutives, **Tiff** and **Tiffie**, exist.

Tiffie: see **Tiffany**

Tilda: see **Matilda**

Tillie: see **Tilly**

Tilly Independently adopted diminutive of **Matilda**. Variant spelling, **Tillie**, was also formerly found, as in famous silent movie *Tillie's Punctured Romance* (1914).

Tina Independent adoption of diminutive of names ending -*tina*, such as **Christina**, **Clementina**, and **Martina**. Few variants or diminutives are in use, although alternate spelling, **Teena**, exists.

Tish: see **Letitia**

Tisha: see **Letitia**

Titia: see **Letitia**

Titty Independently adopted diminutive of **Letitia**. No regular variants.

Toni Either independently adopted diminutive of **Antonia**, or feminine equivalent of **Tony**. Few regular variants exist, although **Tony** is sometimes found.

Tony: see **Toni**

Topsey: see **Topsy**

Topsie: see **Topsy**

Topsy Said to derive from "topsail." Variant spellings, **Topsey** and **Topsie**, have been recorded.

Tottie: see **Charlotte**

Totty: see **Charlotte**

Trace: see **Tracy**

Tracey: see **Tracy**

Tracie: see **Tracy**

Tracy Either from surname, or independently adopted diminutive of **Theresa**. Variant spellings, **Tracey** and **Tracie**, exist, with the former as for British actress Tracey Ullman (born 1954). Diminutive is **Trace**.

Tricia: see **Patricia**

Trish: see **Patricia**

Trisha: see **Patricia**

Trixi: see **Trixie**

Trixie Independently adopted diminutive of **Beatrice** or **Beatrix**. Alternate spelling, **Trixi**, exists.

Trudi: see **Trudy**

Trudie: see **Gertrude** and **Trudy**

Trudy Independently adopted diminutive of **Gertrude** or **Ermintrude**. Variant spellings include **Trudi** and **Trudie**.

Una Irish name (properly *Úna*), perhaps derived from *uan*, "lamb," but also associated with Latin *una*, "one," and so equated with **Unity**. **Oona** is a related name.

Unice: see **Eunice**

Unity From standard word, regarded as a quasi-virtue. No regular variants.

Urse: see **Ursula**

Ursie: see **Ursula**

Ursula From Latin name, itself diminutive of *ursa*, "she-bear." No regular variants, apart from diminutives, **Urse** and **Ursie**.

Val: see **Valeria** and **Valerie**

Valeria Feminine form of Roman clan name *Valerius*, itself probably based on *valere*, "to be healthy" or "to be strong." Diminutive, where name is used, is normally **Val**.

Valerie French form of **Valeria**. Variant spelling, **Valery**, exists, and usual diminutive is **Val**.

Valery: see **Valerie**

Vanessa Name devised by Jonathan Swift in eighteenth century from that of close friend Esther Vanhomrigh, based on first syllables of her surname and first name. (Name is mistakenly thought by some to mean "butterfly," from scientific name, *Vanessa*, of red admiral genus, but this predates woman's name and is probably from name of Greek goddess *Phānēs*.) Variant spelling, **Venessa**, exists, and diminutives include **Nessa**, **Nessie** (in independent use), and **Vanny**.

Vanny: see **Vanessa**

Venessa: see **Vanessa**

Venetia Perhaps from Latin name of Venice, suggested by similar name **Florence**. Few regular variants.

Vera Russian name, meaning "faith," but also happening to coincide with Latin *vera*, "true." (Russian equivalents of "triple virtue" names, **Faith**, **Hope**, and **Charity** are *Vera*,

Nadezhda, and *Lyubov.*) Virtually no variants or diminutives exist, unless Russian **Verochka** is used.

Verena Perhaps form of **Vera**, interpreted as "true" rather than "faith." No regular variants.

Verity From standard word, treated as near-virtue (truth). Few regular variants.

Verna Either from Latin *verna,* "spring," or feminine equivalent of **Vernon**. Few regular variants.

Verochka: see **Vera**

Verona Either shortened form of **Veronica** or from Italian town (compare to **Florence** and **Venetia**). Few regular variants.

Veronica Latin adaptation of *Berenice* (earlier form of **Bernice**), influenced by Church Latin phrase *vera icon,* "true image" (of which name is anagram), referring to legend which tells that after St. Veronica wiped Christ's face she found an image of it imprinted onto the cloth. In modern times it is sometimes linked with plant name or regarded as a variant of **Verona**. French variant, **Véronique,** is sometimes found. Diminutives include **Nicky** (in independent use, though usually from **Nicola**) and **Ronnie.**

Véronique: see **Veronica**

Vesta From Latin name of Roman goddess of hearth and fire, itself from Greek *hestia,* "hearth" (shrine of household gods). Few regular variants.

Vi: see **Vida, Viola, Violet, Vivien,** and **Vivienne**

Vic: see **Victoria**

Vick: see **Victoria**

Vicki Independently adopted diminutive of **Victoria**. Variant spellings include **Vickie**, **Vicky**, and **Vikki**, with the last of these as for singer Vikki Carr (born 1942).

Vickie: see **Vicki** and **Victoria**

Vicky: see **Vicki** and **Victoria**

Victoria Feminine of Latin name *Victorius*, strongly influenced by *victoria*, "victory," and now usually regarded as female equivalent of **Victor**. **Vicki** is diminutive variant in independent use. Others include: **Vic**, **Vick**, **Vickie**, **Vicky**, **Vikki**, and **Vita**.

Vida Independently adopted diminutive of **Davida**, variant of **Davina**. Diminutive, **Vi**, is found.

Vida: see **Davina**

Vikki: see **Vicki** and **Victoria**

Vinnie: see **Lavinia**

Vinny: see **Lavinia**

Viola Originally from Latin *viola*, "violet," but later associated with English plant name and with **Violet**. Variant, **Violetta**, is a related independent name. Diminutive, **Vi**, exists.

Violet From the flower. Diminutive, **Violetta**, is directly related. More usual diminutive is **Vi**.

Violetta Italian diminutive, independently adopted, of **Viola**. No regular variants.

Virginia Feminine form of Roman clan name *Virginius*

(compare to **Virgil**), said to derive from Latin *virgo*, genitive *virginis*, "maiden." Common diminutive is **Ginny.**

Vita: see **Victoria**

Viv: see **Vivian, Vivien,** and **Vivienne**

Vivian Female adoption of male name **Vivian.** Variant spellings in independent use are **Vivien** and **Vivienne.** Usual diminutive is **Viv.**

Vivie: see **Vivien**

Vivien Feminine form of male name **Vivian.** Variant spellings are **Vivian** and **Vivienne,** both in independent use. Usual diminutives are **Vi, Viv,** and **Vivie.**

Vivienne French form of **Vivien.** Diminutives **Vi** and **Viv** exist.

Viviette Alteration of **Vivienne** with French diminutive suffix *-ette* as in **Lynette.** Few established variants.

Vonnie: see **Yvonne**

Wanda Probably of Slavonic origin, related to ethnic name *Wend*. In modern times felt to be variant of **Wendy**. Few variants.

Wend: see **Wendy**

Wendi: see **Wendy**

Wendy Popularly said to be invention of English writer J.M. Barrie for central character in play *Peter Pan* (1904), derived from nickname "Fwendy-Wendy," but could equally be independently adopted diminutive of **Gwendolen**. Spelling variant, **Wendi,** sometimes found, with usual diminutive, **Wend**.

Whitney Female adoption of male name **Whitney**. Few established variants.

Wilhelmina Feminine form of German *Wilhelm* (**William**). Variant spelling, **Williamina,** occurs, as for astronomer Williamina Fleming (1857–1911). Diminutives **Mina, Willa,** and **Wilma** are in independent use.

Willa Independently adopted diminutive of **Wilhelmina**. Few regular variants.

Williamina: see **Wilhelmina**

Wilma Independently adopted diminutive of **Wilhelmina**. Few established variants.

Win: see **Winifred** and **Winnie**

Winifred English version of Welsh name *Gwenfrewi*, from *gwen*, "white," "fair," or "blessed," and *frewi*, "reconciliation": "blessed reconciliation." English form of name was influenced by components of Old English male name *Winfrith*, which are *wine*, "friend," and *frith*, "peace." Diminutives **Freda** and **Winnie** are in independent use. **Win** is also frequently found.

Winnie Independently adopted diminutive of **Winifred**. Diminutive variant, **Win**, exists.

Yas: see **Yasmin**

Yasmin Independently adopted variant of **Jasmine**, based on original Persian or Arabic name with same meaning. Variant spelling, **Yasmine**, occurs. Usual diminutive is **Yas.**

Yasmine: see **Yasmin**

Yola: see **Yolande**

Yolande French name, of obscure ultimate origin. Usual diminutive variant is **Yola**. See also **Iolanthe.**

Yvette Feminine diminutive of French male name *Yves* (**Ivor**), also seen as a diminutive of **Yvonne**. No regular variants.

Yvonne Independently adopted diminutive of French male name *Yves* (**Ivor**). Variant spelling, **Evonne**, perhaps influenced by **Eve** (but also avoiding awkward "Y"), promoted by Australian tennis player Evonne Cawley (born 1951). Diminutive, **Vonnie**, exists.

Zara Either Arabic name, from *zahr*, "flower," or rare independently adopted diminutive of **Sarah**. No regular variants.

Zelda Independently adopted diminutive of **Griselda**. No regular variants.

Zena Perhaps shortened form of **Zenobia**, independently adopted diminutive of **Rosina**, or (according to some) from Persian word meaning "woman." No regular variants.

Zenobia Greek name, feminine form of *Zēnobios*, from *Zeus*, poetic genitive *Zēnos*, "Zeus" (greatest of Greek gods), and *bios*, "life": "life of Zeus." No regular variants.

Zoe From Greek word, meaning "life." Main variant is spelling, **Zoë** (with dieresis), but **Zowie** also occasionally occurs.

Zoë: see **Zoe**

Zola Apparently variant of **Zoë**, perhaps subconsciously suggested by surname of French writer Emile Zola (1840–1902). No regular variants.

Zona Perhaps alteration of **Zena**. No regular variants.

Zora Perhaps adaptation of biblical place name Zorah. Variant spelling is **Zorah**, found as name of professional bridesmaid in Gilbert and Sullivan comic opera *Ruddigore* (1887).

Zorah: see **Zora**

Zowie: see **Zoe**

Zuleika Persian name, frequently found in poetry, and probably meaning "brilliant beauty." No regular variants.